Television and Criticism

Edited by Solange Davin and Rhona Jackson

Television and Criticism

Edited by Solange Davin and Rhona Jackson

intellect Bristol, UK / Chicago, USA

First Published in the UK in 2008 by
Intellect Books, The Mill, Parnall Road, Fishponds, Bristol, BS16 3JG, UK

First published in the USA in 2008 by
Intellect Books, The University of Chicago Press, 1427 E. 60th Street, Chicago,
IL 60637, USA

Cover Design: Gabriel Solomons
Copy Editor: Holly Spradling
Typesetting: Mac Style, Nafferton, E. Yorkshire

ISBN 978-1-84150-147-5

Printed and bound in Great Britain by The Charlesworth Group, Wakefield

CONTENTS

INTRODUCTION

Solange Davin and Rhona Jackson

The number of research studies into television is vast, and their variety of foci demonstrates the diverse ways it has been understood in academic terms. How television has been theorized has depended on whether it has been approached as, say, visual medium or cultural form, public broadcaster or domestic reception, institution of power or democratizing force.

For instance, Thomas Elsaesser (1969)[1] contended that, despite film and television both being visual media, because film was received in the cinema and television in the home, their conditions of viewing determined that the audience experience varied accordingly. Then, John Ellis's *Visual Fictions* (1982)[2] outlined how the institutions, texts and audiences for film and television operated and overlapped. And, in 1991, John Caughie[3] argued that the finite nature of film and the flow of television were sufficiently dissimilar to demand a corresponding difference in critical approach and suggested that a more effective understanding of television could be gained were it approached in terms less of text than of reception, of consumption rather than production.

Alternatively, Raymond Williams (1974)[4] advocated that television was more than visual medium, and that television as cultural form should be the centre of attention. As well as being the first to propose the concept of 'flow' to explain how television programming was structured, and, accordingly, how viewers related to it, he argued that television's power derives from it being a public medium received in the domestic sphere. Whilst a tool of popular culture as well as a cultural form itself, it is a repository of texts and *the* influential conveyor of meanings and messages, which audiences watch, receive and engage with.

Additionally, studies into television as institution have concentrated on power and control,[5] technological developments and the resulting fragmentation of audiences, and, most recently, globalization[6] and regional/local television.[7]

Research into television audiences has developed from the very early effects research heavily influenced by Robert Merton's *Mass Persuasion* (1946),[8] which has been resurrected on a regular basis, usually as a result of moral panics following particularly tragic incidents such as the murder of James Bulger in 1992. However, whilst American effects studies have for over twenty years concluded that television is likely to have negative effects on 'vulnerable' viewers,[9] UK research remains inconclusive.[10] As a response to these perceived failings of effects research, the uses and gratifications audience model grew in popularity, UK researchers in particular choosing to begin with the premise of the active audience who purposefully select what they want to watch to fulfil specific needs.[11] Plus, research has been undertaken into the influence that social class[12] and gender[13] has on viewers, and how television traditionally targeted a family audience, viewers responding according to their role in the family unit and family dynamics.[14]

Critics have summarized many of the approaches to television. Robert C. Allen's *Channels of Discourse: Reassembled* in 1992 compiled a number of perspectives, including, for example, articles on television as genre[15] and as ideology.[16] Following this, John Corner (1997: 249)[17] maintained that theories about television fall broadly into one of four categories: 'representation, medium, institution and process'. And in 1998, Christine Geraghty and David Lusted's *The Television Studies Book* examined the nature of Television Studies,[18] with Charlotte Brunsdon posing the question, 'What is the "Television" of Television Studies?'[19]

There have been publications on specific programmes and genres.[20] Plus, studies have shown how television can be understood in terms of its value to society. So, for instance, books about how to apply theories of Cultural Studies[21] all include television as a key component to exemplify how the theories work.

Assorted books and articles on television, therefore, abound. So, what is the place of this volume? It is fair to say that the majority of people would acknowledge that television is central to contemporary society, so this collection demonstrates that, correspondingly, television criticism has become an important focus for a variety of critical applications. Other compilations have drawn together studies which demonstrate the diversity of what can be studied in terms of Television Studies. This book points to the number of different disciplines which Television Studies has been influenced by and can draw on in order to explain its centrality to Cultural Studies in general, research into media influence, and ways in which the television audience can be approached which do not rely solely on the effects or Uses and Gratifications traditions.

Thus, the chapters in this volume illustrate ways of approaching the study of television whilst also establishing the critical place of Television Studies in the wider locus of cultural criticism. Although there are, inevitably, overlaps throughout, we have attempted to present chapters in an order which has a reasonable logic. As it is likely that the first thing most people think of when discussing television is 'What's on?', the central focus of the first three chapters is television programmes. There follows three chapters which illuminate how certain television critical approaches have developed by integrating theories from other disciplines. And the final three chapters explore the role of contemporary television in terms of the interface between 'individualism' and 'the social'.

The texts discussed in chapters 1, 2 and 3 illustrate the contemporary relationship of literature to television. They demonstrate how criticism can reveal both the significance of television programmes' literary origins and their influence in terms of popular understanding of contemporary culture in general. Len Platt begins with 'Our Common Cultural Heritage', where he looks at how reproductions of classic literary *oeuvres* on the small screen in turn reproduce conservative societal and literary values. Beginning with Jane Austen, he seeks to understand what might be involved in the practice of reproducing 'Literature' in the modern, industrial and visual form that is television. Challenging notions that the classic serial simply reproduces the novel text in a neutral form, Platt sees the televised novels as a modernist intervention that reconvenes the novel as 'safe pleasure' and historical spectacle. At the same time as the televised novel 'smoothes out' many of the contradictions, complexities and idiosyncrasies of the written text, it becomes more directly ideological, a crucial means of reproducing conservative notions of gender identity, class and nation for the maintenance of a highly traditional version of the literary canon.

Then, Dorothy Hobson discusses how the roots of what is often considered as the archetypal television form – the soap opera – can be found in traditional literature, which may help explore the genre's universal popularity. 'Aspects of Soap Opera and Other Stories' identifies the origin of soap opera and continuous series, two major forms of drama production which dominate national and global television, in oral literature, folk tale, the literary realist writers of the eighteenth and nineteenth centuries, the serial novels of Charles Dickens and the domestic and personal detail of the novels of authors like Jane Austen or George Eliot. Hobson applies to soap opera literary theories such as Ian Watt's notion of the individual and the universal, E. M. Forster's characteristics of the novel, the *Bildungsroman* and K. L. Walton's theories of 'Pretending Belief' which may help to explain the popularity and universal appeal of the genre.

Curtis Breight examines the complex relationship of UK and US TV through the analysis of an after-school programme with Shakespearian overtones. He analyses the made-for-American-television film *My Dark Lady* as one obscure, albeit key, example of how traditional English culture and its highest exponent, William Shakespeare, constitute the central contribution to an otherwise political, military and economic relationship dominated by the United States from as far back as World War II. *My Dark Lady*, a film designed for 'after-school' impressionable viewers who are taught that the 'Mother Country' of England is still relevant, even indispensable, to upward mobility in cash- and class-stratified America, epitomizes how 'disabled' Americans, in this case disenfranchised African Americans, can rise in an oppressive system by combining their efforts with the cultural talent of a failed British Shakespearean actor on the run from the law.

All chapters demonstrate how television criticism has evolved by 'borrowing' from other disciplines, chapters 4, 5 and 6 pointing up how this works in three specific ways: historiography and TV; film theory and TV; and film spectatorship theory, TV audience studies and reader response theory. Anne Wales, for instance, questions how televised historical representations are constructed according to rhetorical strategies shaping social memory and imagination. She explores the possibilities for using historiographical frameworks to investigate the reflexive relationship of television and history as they emerged from developments in the 1980s and 90s. Within critical discourse, a key debate has foregrounded the relationship between historical events and their interpretation within history writing through narratives and tropes. Wales argues that the notion of meta-history was utilized within critical historiography to examine what it meant to think historically and how social memory shapes the historical imagination. The challenges of postmodernism brought notions of understanding historical events as a form of discourse or in terms of subjectivities of the historical actors. More recently, there has been re-engagement with history as a process including consideration of cause and effect. Wales suggests that television texts, like history writing, are constructed according to rhetorical strategies and have been key elements in the late twentieth and twenty-first centuries in shaping both social memory and the historical imagination.

Barton Palmer, then discusses how the move from big to small screen altered *Dragnet*, an early American police series and confined its voice to a simple conservative viewpoint. *Dragnet* was one of the longest-running and most acclaimed American 'television noir' series of the 1950s, adapted from radio. Palmer traces its critical and popular reception to establish how it is similar to, yet significantly diverges from the reception of *film noir* which provides the series with its 'realistic' police procedural model. Archival resources and contemporary reviews identify what were, for critics, the key elements of the genre/series formula. He concludes that early television was more ideologically conservative than its big screen counterpart, and that where the police procedural *film noir* is often a fractured text controlled by several perspectives, *Dragnet* adopts a unitary viewpoint, that of the police, although its tone and style reflect the world-weariness associated with the *film noir* criminal.

And Rhona Jackson proposes the concept of the Skilled Viewer which integrates the multiple layers of the reception process. This is a theoretical model of interpretation to aid television audience research, combining literary criticism's Reader-Response theory, film spectatorship theory and the Uses and Gratifications approach to television audiences. Jackson draws also on findings from fieldwork research into fandom and audience responses. The resulting model can explain viewers' responses emotionally, intellectually and as social beings influenced by the context of viewing. Thus, the Skilled

Viewer incorporates learned interpretive customs and internalized social experience, hypothesizing a social, gendered being whose viewing experience is structured by social position, gender, age, interests and by a common comprehension of the influence of such factors/positions. It encompasses the social nature of the viewing experience and a notion of viewing competence. The Skilled Viewer actively views television for a variety of reasons, understanding/using the language of the visual text and the conventions associated with television broadcasting, production and programme construction.

Finally, chapters 7, 8 and 9 explore how, by adopting and adapting strategies from other disciplines, television has emerged as a major influence on viewer subjectivity and perception of self. Felix Thompson looks at how British television dramas have integrated the aesthetics of traditional drama fiction and reality television, drawing on the examples of the series *Queer as Folk* and *This Life*. He questions whether the critical approaches to television which evolved in the 1960s and '70s are still applicable today or whether the changes from public service values to market-driven consumer individualism and from a few channels to a multi-channel environment have resulted in the obsolescence of these critical categories. Thompson examines the extent to which the open-ended possibilities for self-fashioning intersect with crises of emotional and material scarcity for which the more traditional aesthetics modes of naturalism and melodrama are invoked. What emerges, he argues, is a dialogue between the discourses of self-transformation closer to reality television and the sense of limits and socially regulated scarcity, conveyed by the more traditional aesthetics modes of dramatic fiction.

Then, Michael Skovmand examines how contemporary television comedies address the worries of their pre-midlife single viewers. He focuses on the three American series *Friends*, *Ally McBeal* and, particularly, *Seinfeld*. He argues that *Seinfeld* can be seen as a 'Comedy of Manners' in that it affords a particular point of entry into contemporary mediatized negotiations of 'civility'. That is, it is concerned with the way in which individual desires and values interface with the conventions and standard of family, peer groups and society at large. The apparent triviality of subject matter and the hermetic appearance of the groups depicted may deceive the unsuspecting media researcher into believing that these comedies are indeed 'about nothing'. Yet, it can be seen to derive its popularity from the way it addresses central concerns of its audience. In other words, *Seinfeld* can be understood as a site of ongoing negotiations of behavioural anxieties within post-teenage, pre-midlife singles culture – a culture which in many ways could be argued to articulate central concerns of society as a whole.

In 'I've been searching my soul tonight' Jill Barker's empirical study of *Ally McBeal* audiences begins from a consideration of responses, exploring expectations and viewing patterns through a questionnaire technique. The questionnaire explores Jardine's suggestion that enjoyment of the programme is directly related to viewer subjectivity. Barker moves from these results to consider the programme's characteristic attitudes to the human body, arguing that Bakhtin's theories of the grotesque provides insights into the exaggerated, and sometimes even repulsive ways that the body is represented. Barker suggests that ritual and convention are frequently derided explicitly within the programme's plot lines and scripts and implicitly by the *mise-en-scène* and surrealist graphics. Form here can be revealingly read as function. The carnivalesque modes in turn invite a reading of the programme's subversions of contention as metaphoric of a more generally troubled/disrupted vision of individual identity and of social structures generally.

Notes

1. 'Narrative Cinema and Audience Orientated Aesthetics' (written in 1969), in Bennett, Tony et al., (eds), 1981: *Popular Film and Television*, London: BFI/Open University.
2. *Visible Fictions – cinema – television – video*, London: Routledge.
3. 'Adorno's Reproach: Repetition, Difference and Television Genre', in *Screen*, 32: 2.
4. *Television: Technology and Cultural Form*, London: Methuen.
5. Cf. Gerbner, George; Mowlana, Hamid and Schiller, Herbert (eds), 1996: *Invisible Crises: What Conglomerate Media Control Means for America and the World*, Boulder, CO: Westview Press; Couldry, Nick, 2003: *Media Rituals*, London: Routledge.
6. Cf. Barker, Chris, 1999: *Television, Globalisation and Cultural Identities*, Maidenhead: Open University Press; Flew, Terry, 2007: *Understanding Global Media*, Basingstoke: Palgrave Macmillan.
7. Corner, John; Harvey, Sylvia; and Robins, Keith (eds), 1993: *The Regions, The Nations and the BBC*, London: British Film Institute; Scannell, Paddy, 2000: 'Public Service Broadcasting: The History of a Concept', in Buscombe, Edward (ed.), *British Television: A Reader*, Oxford: Oxford University Press; Harvey, Sylvia, 2004: *Defining, Maintaining and Strengthening Public Service Broadcasting*, submission to Ofcom Review of Public Service Television Broadcasting;; Rushton, Dave (ed), 1993: *CITIZEN TELEVISION: a local dimension to Public Service Broadcasting*, Edinburgh: John Libbey & Institute of Local Television; Rushton, Dave (ed), 2005: *LOCAL TELEVISION RENEWED: essays on local television 1994–2005*, Edinburgh: School Press for the Institute of Local Television; Rushton, Dave (ed), 1993: *CITIZEN TELEVISION: a local dimension to Public Service Broadcasting*, Edinburgh: John Libbey & Institute of Local Television.
8. *Mass Persuasion: The Social Psychology of a War Bond Drive*, in *The American Journal of Psychology*, 51.6: 541–557.
9. Cf. Gerbner, George and Signorielli, Nancy, 1988: *Violence and Terror in the Media: An Annotated Bibliography*, Westport, CT: Greenwood Press.
10. Cf. Cumberbatch, Guy: *A Measure of Uncertainty: The Effects of the Mass Media*, London: Libbey; Barker, Martin and Petley, Julian, 2001: *Ill Effects: The Media Violence Debate*, London, Routledge.
11. Cf. McQuail, Denis (ed), 1972: *Sociology of Mass Communications*, Harmondsworth: Penguin Books Ltd.; McQuail, Denis, 1993: *Mass Communication Theory*, London: Sage; McQuail, Denis, 2002: *Mass Communications Theory: A Reader*, London: Sage.
12. Cf. Morley, David, 1980: *The Nationwide Audience*, London: BFI; Morley, David, 1981: 'Nationwide: A Critical Postscript', in *Screen*, 30, 2: 6–18.

13. Gray, Ann, 1986: 'Behind Closed Doors: Video Recorders in the Home', in Baehr, Helen and Dyer, Gill (eds): *Boxed In: Women and Television*, London: Pandora; Morley, David, 1986: *Family Television: Cultural Power and Domestic Leisure*, London: Routledge.

14. Cf. Morley, David, 1986: *Family Television: Cultural Power and Domestic Leisure*, London: Routledge; Walkerdine, Valerie, 1986: 'Video Replay: Families, Films and Fantasy', in Alvarado, Manuel and Thompson, J. G. (eds): *The Media Reader*, London: BFI; Starke, Nicola, 1998: *A Case Study of How Different People in the Same Household Use Television*, http://www.aber.ac.uk/media/Students/nas9601.html.

15. By Jane Feuer in Robert C. Allen (ed.), 1992: *Channels of Discourse, Reassembled* (ed.), London, Routledge.

16. By Mimi White in Robert C. Allen (ed.) ibid.

17. 'Television in theory', in *Media, Culture and Society, 19: 2*.

18. *The Television Studies Book*, 1988, London: Arnold.

19. Cf. also Crisell, Andrew, 2006: *A Study of Modern Television: Thinking Inside the Box*, Basingstoke: Palgrave Macmillan.

20. Soaps in particular have been the topic of many studies. Cf. Buckingham, David, 1987, *Public Secrets*, London: BFI; Seiter, Ellen et al. (eds), 1989, *Remote Control: Television, Audiences, and Cultural Power*, London: Routledge; Brunsdon, Charlotte, 2000: *The Feminist, the Housewife and the Soap Opera*, Oxford: The Clarendon Press. Plus, books about genre in general, e.g. Creeber, Glen, 2001: *The Television Genre Book*, London: BFI.

21. Cf. Storey, John, 1992: *An Introductory Guide to Cultural theory and Popular Culture*, London: Harvester Wheatsheaf; Strinati, Dominic, 1995: *An Introduction to Theories of Popular Culture*, London: Routledge; Strinati, Dominic, 2000: , London: Routledge.

References

Allen, Robert. C, 1992: *Channels of Discourse: Reassembled – Television and Contemporary Criticism*, (2nd edn) London: Routledge.

Alvarado, Manuel and Thompson, J. G. (eds), 1986: *The Media Reader*, London: BFI.

Baehr, Helen and Dyer, Gill (eds), 1986: *Boxed In: Women and Television*, London: Pandora.

Barker, Chris, 1999: *Television, Globalisation and Cultural Identities*, Maidenhead: Open University Press.

Barker, Martin and Petley, Julian, 2001: *Ill Effects: The Media Violence Debate*, London: Routledge.

Brunsdon, Charlotte, 2000: *The Feminist, the Housewife and the Soap Opera*, Oxford: The Clarendon Press.

Buckingham, David, 1987: *Public Secrets*, London: BFI.

Buscombe, Edward (ed.), 2000: *British Television: A Reader*, Oxford: Oxford University Press.

Harvey, Sylvia, 2004: *Defining, Maintaining and Strengthening Public Service Broadcasting*, submission to Ofcom Review of Public Service Television Broadcasting.

Bennett, Tony et al. (eds), 1981: *Popular Film and Television*, London: BFI/Open University.

Caughie, John, 1991: 'Adorno's Reproach: Repetition, Difference and Television Genre', in *Screen*, 32: 2.

Corner, John, 1997: 'Television in theory', in *Media, Culture and Society, 19: 2*.

Corner, John; Harvey, Sylvia; and Robins, Keith (eds), 1993: *The Regions, The Nations and the BBC*, London: British Film Institute.

Couldry, Nick, 2003: *Media Rituals*, London: Routledge.

Creeber, Glen, 2001: *The Television Genre Book*, London: BFI.

Crisell, Andrew, 2006: *A Study of Modern Television: Thinking Inside the Box*, Basingstoke: Palgrave Macmillan.

Cumberbatch, Guy: *A Measure of Uncertainty: The Effects of the Mass Media*, London: Libbey.

Ellis, John, 1982: *Visible Fictions – cinema – television – video*, London: Routledge.

Flew, Terry, 2007: *Understanding Global Media*, Basingstoke: Palgrave Macmillan.

Geraghty, Christine and Lusted, David (eds), 1988: *The Television Studies Book*, London: Arnold.

Gerbner, George and Signorielli, Nancy, 1988: *Violence and Terror in the Media: an Annotated Bibliography*, Westport, CT: Greenwood Press.

Gerbner, George; Mowlana, Hamid and Schiller, Herbert (eds), 1996: *Invisible Crises: What Conglomerate Media Control Means for America and the World*, Boulder, CO: Westview Press

McQuail, Denis (ed.), 1972: *Sociology of Mass Communications*, Harmondsworth: Penguin Books Ltd.

——, 1993: *Mass Communication Theory*, London: Sage.

——, 2002: *Mass Communications Theory: A Reader*, London: Sage.

Merton, Robert, 1946: *Mass Persuasion: The Social Psychology of a War Bond Drive*, in *The American Journal of Psychology*, 51.6: 541–557.

Morley, David, 1980: *The Nationwide Audience*, London: BFI.

——, 1981: 'Nationwide: A Critical Postscript', in *Screen*, 30, 2: 6–18.

——, 1986: *Family Television: Cultural Power and Domestic Leisure*, London: Routledge.

——, 1992: *Television, Audiences and Cultural Studies*, London: Routledge.

Rushton, Dave (ed.), 1993: *CITIZEN TELEVISION: a local dimension to Public Service Broadcasting*, Edinburgh: John Libbey & Institute of Local Television.

—— (ed.), 2005: *LOCAL TELEVISION RENEWED: essays on local television 1994–2005*, Edinburgh: School Press for the Institute of Local Television.

Seiter, Ellen et al. (eds), 1989: *Remote Control: Television, Audiences, and Cultural Power*, London: Routledge.

Starke, Nicola, 1998: *A Case Study of How Different People in the Same Household Use Television*, http://www.aber.ac.uk/media/Students/nas9601.html.

Storey, John, 1992: *An Introductory Guide to Cultural theory and Popular Culture*, London: Harvester Wheatsheaf.

Strinati, Dominic, 1995: *An Introduction to Theories of Popular Culture*, London: Routledge.

——, 2000: *An Introduction to Studying Popular Culture*, London: Routledge.

Williams, Raymond, 1974: *Television: Technology and Cultural Form*, London: Methuen.

Our Common Cultural Heritage: Classic Novels and English Television

Len Platt

Modern media have used the novel as a source for drama from the beginning. The production companies responsible for reproducing 'classic novels' have been attracted not just by the ready-made plots and characters, but, also, perhaps especially in English film and television,[1] by the status of canonical texts that have a virtually unassailable currency in terms of cultural value. Indeed these two elements are inseparable, with the 'filmability' of the classic novel being shaped and determined by its high status in cultural terms. As the cultural form *par excellence* of the educated classes, the novel gives film-makers not just a stock of stories and memorable heroes and villains, but also a direct line to prestige. It is not surprising that the adaptation of the novel to film has been seen as playing a considerable part in establishing the reputation of mainstream film as a serious and important 'popular' culture.[2]

The BBC, a key institutional force in bringing classic literature to a wider modern audience, began its involvement in the 1920s – the 1928 radio production of *The Three Musketeers* is usually seen as a landmark in this respect.[3] Further radio productions of nineteenth-century novels swiftly followed, with the works of such writers as Austen, Dickens, Scott, Trollope and Thackeray, forming the staple of radio serialization. The first classic serial shown by BBC television was a six-part version of Trollope's *The Warden* (1951). Thereafter classic serials became a regular feature in BBC television scheduling. From 1963 to 1979 there was a separate BBC department set up specifically for the production of serials generally (called the Serials Department), and it was here that the hugely successful classic serials of that period were produced – possibly the most talked about classic serial of all, *The Forsyte Saga*, for example, 'reached an average weekly audience of 15,500,000 in Britain, and by 1970 the BBC could boast that it had been watched by more than 160,000,000 people in 45 countries.'[4]

It is possible to regard 1951–1981 as something of 'a golden age' for television serializations of classic novels, but their appearance has continued more or less evenly to the current time and they have been exported all over the world. The 1972 version of *Emma*, for instance, with all its romanticized images of early-nineteenth-century England and Englishness, was apparently keenly sought after in such postcolonial environments as Australia, Bahrain, Ireland, Kenya, Malaysia and Singapore, as well as Iceland, Romania, Hungary and Sweden.[5] There was a brief period from the mid 1980s to early 90s when the popularity of classic serials seemed to wane, corresponding to an accelerated Americanization of British television – not that American corporations have been unsupportive of the English classic serial. Much of the budget for Granada's 1977 production of *Hard Times* came from New York's Public Broadcasting station WNET-TV,[6] a relatively early example of transnational funding operations that are now standard – Arts and Entertainment New York, for instance, was the co-producer of the 1995 BBC version of *Pride and Prejudice*. The later 90s, however, did see a renewed interest in the viability of the classic serial, with the emergence of new writers – Andrew Davies being one obvious and eminent representative here – making strong reputations as interpreters of the great novel tradition. Similarly new popular actors found mileage in what is often understood to be a characteristic style of English performance and one of the quintessential English cultural forms.

From its earliest days to the present day, then, television has systematically both adapted and adopted the 'classic' English novel. The classic serial has been a standard feature in television programming, especially in BBC schedules. Indeed, although other English production companies have invested in classic serials, the relationship between the BBC and this particular form remains intimate[7] and has contributed to the sense that the classic serial is not just a celebration, but a continuation of a standard of high cultural value that is frequently nationalized, or racialized. Thus an eminent theorist of television, writing in 1993, applauds the success of one such serialization on the grounds that it supported 'the notion that Britain had the best television in the world, certainly the best television drama', without too much concern over what it means to construct cultural value in such a way.[8]

Perhaps the most costly programmes to produce, these modern reconstructions of classic novels remain highly prestigious, then, and therefore central to the BBC's earliest and most celebrated mission to 'inform, educate and entertain.'[9] For all its critics, the serialized classic novel is still a key component in English television's much vaunted, if now diminished, reputation for high quality. Strangely, given its status and relative longevity as a 'popular' cultural form, there have been relatively few attempts at theorizing this phenomenon, at least as far as the formal academy is concerned – a fact that renders this current essay provisional in some respects and quite generalized in its approach. With something of a focus on televised versions of Austen's novels, it considers classic novel serializations and the issue of cultural value from a perspective governed by Cultural Studies, and influenced by contemporary critical approaches to literature. This does not much involve arguing for or against the standard of individual serializations, or of the genre generally – although, inevitably, some dispositions do creep in in this respect. Nor is the intention to compare specific novels against films for quality, or to participate seriously in the long-standing debate over whether the classic serial 'corrupts' the novel tradition or is educative in bringing it to a wider audience. The primary interest, rather, is in the larger question of what it means to reproduce 'Literature' (meaning the canon and all the values attached to it)[10] in a modern, industrial and visual form. The emphasis is not on ascribing cultural value, but on understanding the complex dynamics that have developed between a modern contemporary culture and the traditional culture that has supported it. In the first instance, this involves some interrogation of the general relationships that exist, or are commonly supposed to exist, between the classic serial and its prototype.

Verisimilitude – the spectacle of likeness

Classic serials respond to a mimesis imperative in two distinct ways. Firstly, the televised classic has to be seen to be 'faithful' to the original text. This is not simply a matter of respect for the master copy, as it were; it is also a question of responding to an imagined sense of relationship between the reader and the classic novel. Viewers, according to television legend, expect and demand utter faithfulness to the fictions they love. They will, allegedly, be quick to complain about deviations from the original, although one suspects that for every viewer who protests about a classic serial on this score, there must be millions who miss such divergences, or have no feelings about them at all. The idea that there is a powerful interest 'out there', avidly protecting the virtue of English literature from the ravages of popularization, is, to a large extent, a myth which serves a dual function. It both underwrites the 'authenticity' of classic serialization, because it places the form under such apparently strict surveillance and authorizes its claim to contemporary relevance. Thus the media interest generated in rumoured sex scenes in the 1995 version of *Pride and Prejudice*. The 'exposure' of the awful liberties that long-haired television makers were apparently about to inflict on a national treasure did no harm to the viewing figures of the show, but whether it reflected a real concern of 'the British public' must be highly doubtful. Whatever, makers of classic serials have frequently expressed what they see as their responsibility to 'Literature' and its readers and this invariably implicates the idea of remaining 'true' to the text. Against those who understand the televised classic novel as 'aerosol versions of great work'[11] constituting a 'hollowing out of our common cultural heritage',[12] the makers of these serials, and some critical traditions, talk of an implied cultural continuity, of honest, professional and creative attempts at 'getting it right', and of bringing high culture to a wider constituency, albeit in a modern, commercial form.[13]

Secondly, almost all classic serializations become costume dramas. As well as re-creating the novel, they must also reproduce the historical period in which the novel was written or set. Since classic novels are, overwhelmingly in the collective mind of television companies, nineteenth-century novels, the recreation of the novel means the recreation of a historical culture. Sometimes this is achieved in very approximate ways and involves little more than a general Victorianization that stands in for 'old England' (see, for instance, the very crude version of Victorian London constructed in Granada Television's 1999 version of *Oliver Twist* or the more marginal 1980 version of *Pride and Prejudice*, scripted by Fay Weldon, which seems reasonably convincing in terms of dress and interiors but, even to the inexpert ear and eye, particularly poor, even disinterested, when it comes to early-nineteenth-century music and dance). Other shows, however, have gone to great lengths to get the reproduction as plausible as possible. In the 1995 production of *Pride and Prejudice* substantial resources were devoted to the antiquarian instinct, with researchers being employed to find out about a great range of aspects of landed society in the early nineteenth century, from the obvious signifiers (buildings, dress, hairstyles, carriages, soft furnishings and so on) to the less so (fashions in garden flowers, the intricacies of ballroom etiquette and the protective clothes worn by early-nineteenth-century beekeepers, for example).[14]

In reality, however, neither of these imperatives can be completely fulfilled. Indeed the whole business of 'faithful reproduction', whether of the novel itself or of 'society and culture then' must be loose and highly provisional and involves a great deal of sleight of hand or 'television magic'. As far as the television serial reproducing the novel is concerned, there is the obvious point that film and novel are distinct forms – to put it simply, many textual qualities of the novel do not transfer easily to film, if at all. There have been some critical attempts to argue that film can reproduce the novelistic, with the camera operating as an author discourse or 'metalanguage',[15] but few would now accept such positions, especially with regard to a tradition of televised classic serials which has been so typically homogeneous in style. The result, far from reproducing the stylistic variation of the novel, has been a flattening that erases what is often most interesting about the written text. Even without this manifestation of the commercial reproduction of the novel tradition for a 'mass' audience, however, the film will always be a version of the novel, rather than a 'faithful copy'. It is a distinct medium with a distinct aesthetic, which is why debates about the quality of the film relative to the book and vice versa have so little meaning or impact in terms of critical theory (although analyzing the *version* of a novel produced on film in order to compare textual meaning does seem a reasonable and possibly important critical challenge). The film must be *different* from the book and makers of classic serials know this better than most – which is why they often talk about the freedom of interpretation, as well as the imperative of faithfulness to the original.[16]

Reproducing the 'historical setting' of the novel and its novelist is equally problematic. The practical impossibility of producing absolute accuracy means that this kind of reconstruction, however thoroughly researched and assembled, is always a question of 'avoiding the worst anomalies' and creating a consistent approximation of period that works internally. The skill, as one set designer puts it, is in 'judging just how much liberty you can take.'[17] Moreover, the 'historical setting' of the novel is not somehow divorced from the manufacture of the novel text. It is, itself, a version of history, an interpretation of culture and society with its own emphases, distortion, gaps and inconsistencies. In aiming for a reproduction of the historical dimension, the television serial replicates not 'history itself', as the makers often imply, but the past as it is thought to have been reproduced in fiction. It is an interesting question how indebted our imaginative and critical understanding of the past (of Victorian London, for instance, so much a product of Dickens's fiction, or early-nineteenth-century landed society, organized by Austen as 'England') is shaped and determined by these fictional interventions and the filmic versions that popularize them anew.

The classic serial clearly does involve a strong recognition of 'Literature' – the sheer persistence of the classic serial, and the resource level devoted to producing it, tell us just how viable the status of 'Literature' seems to be in contemporary television culture in Britain and, indeed, worldwide, both in cultural and commercial terms. But it is only in a highly qualified sense that the classic serial reconstructs the specific novel. Nor is it actually 'history' that is celebrated in classic serials, or some unmediated past, but (at least where the reproduction is compelling and consistent) the modern, technological culture that can image the past so splendidly. It is the transforming power of modern culture that is demonstrated and applauded here, or criticized where it fails to be convincing. As so often in modern culture, the facsimile makes the first impression, with the copy being marveled at as copy – another way of making the point that adaptations often consume the memory of novels 'to efface it with the presence of its own images.'[18] For this reason, the education discourse frequently employed by makers of classic serials misses the point in many respects and is misleading. It is not so much 'information', 'knowledge' or 'Culture' that the serializations of classic novels produce, but, rather, a very specific, notionally middlebrow and technologically advanced form of spectacle that is packaged as 'Literature'.

Classic serials and *léscriture*
The suggestion that the classic serial, for all its apparent literariness, functions as high-status eye candy is consistent with some extremely influential theorizations of modern popular culture. For someone like Daniel Bell, following the culture industry theorists, one crucial characteristic of modern culture is its movement away from complex textual meaning and the subsequent reliance on the immediate sensual experience. This has often been understood both in terms of aesthetic decline and of the implications for social order and consent, with the state and corporate life expanding its influence in and through a 'culture industry' whose main function is as soporific. Here astonishment, delight and amazement would become key to the cultural experience, displacing more traditional, cerebral and critical engagements. Hearing and seeing would become more forcefully deployed than listening and 'reading'; extravagant design, spectacular costumes, again in theatre terms, would take over from more complex and literary textual effects. Sights and 'also sounds...[would] become central in the production of meaning and identity', indeed the dominant social outlook of modernity in Bell's *The Cultural Contradictions of Capitalism* is considered to be 'visual', with the characteristic positioning being more outwardly disposed than inwardly regarding.[19]

Now the classic serial is in many ways highly suggestive of a modern culture that is visual and it does exploit the visual spectacle in modern ways. Indeed, inasmuch as it involves the 'translation' of a high-status reading culture into a seeing one, the classic serial stands as a particularly resonant emblem of modern culture in this respect. However, that does not make words and scripts redundant to the televising of the novel. On the contrary, the serialized novel makes an obvious investment in words and word culture. This is partly how the classic serial culture gets its defining character as a particular mediator that manages the traditional/modern and high/low cultural divides. Whatever its investment in the modern, and however visual its interpretation of the original narrative, the classic serial remains notionally intertextual with its prototype and in this sense performs the highly significant balancing act of reconciling modern technological culture with a more traditional privileging of the written word and the 'literary'. In a potentially highly charged and ideological configuration, it purports to make traditional 'quality' meaningful and accessible in modernity and on a 'mass' scale.

The classic serial must remain devoted to the idea of a word culture if it is to exploit the status of 'Literature', which is perhaps one reason why it has so often utilized the services of the most writerly of contemporary writers – Alan Bleasdale, for instance, whose *Oliver Twist* is one of the best televised serials, and Denis Potter, who wrote the 1978 version of *The Mayor of Casterbridge*. What is produced here in the television scripts, however, and whoever the writer may be, is obviously very different from the original novel in terms of language, whether one thinks of language as system, aesthetics or discourse. One obvious distinction between the playscript and the novel is that the playscript is comprised exclusively of dialogue and stage direction. Other 'voices' the novel might adopt – narrative, descriptive, discursive, parodic voices, for instance – are, at best, compromised. The point about such 'dialogic' or multi-vocality is that it is central, not just to the workings of individual novels, but to most contemporary accounts of the novel form and its traditions. In the playscript, however, all this 'fabric' is seriously displaced, if not altogether erased. What remains is not so much the individual text, registering the uniqueness of a novelist and a novel as it articulates against the imagined social world, but, rather, a non-standard dialogue. This latter has a number of key functions. It operates plot (the key organizing principle of adaptation)[20] and characterizations and is supposed to stand in for some notion of the specific literary signature of a canonical writer. It also features as a version of period English. But it is not the authentic novel text. In describing her difficulties memorizing lines for *Pride and Prejudice*, the actress Jennifer Ehle talks misleadingly of learning *Austen's* dialogue and as being like 'learning another language'. Alison Steadman talks in similar terms of finding the language of the show 'very difficult'.[21] Actually they were not learning Austen's language at all, or early-nineteenth-century English (whatever that abstraction might mean) but, rather, generalized approximations of imagined literariness.

It should be emphasized that this gap between the literary text and film is not simply a matter of elements of 'narrative' not translating to filmed dramatic versions. Even the dialogue of classic novels refuses transcription for television, as many writers who undertake adaptation have pointed out. Andrew Davies, for example, has talked about wanting to make Austen's dialogue 'something that could be spoken in the early nineteenth century, but also something you wouldn't find terribly artificial if it were spoken now.'[22] Denis Constanduros is more extreme in this respect, arguing that Austen's dialogue on television would be 'terribly long, stilted and unnatural sounding.'[23] There are, of course, authenticating gestures but most playscript dialogue is usually much altered and often entirely made up. Bleasdale's foregrounding of the 'back-story' of *Oliver Twist* is suggestive here. This works extremely well dramatically, but it is not Dickens. Indeed, it involves nothing less than the creation of a character, the invention of a murder and a whole episode comprised largely of scenes and dialogue that have no counterpart in the Dickens' novel at all. The playscript, then, bears little real resemblance to the novel itself, so much so that it is usually quite impossible to follow a televised serial and the original text in tandem. What we have in the language text of the classic serial, as with the filmed image, is, again, a version which stands in for, somewhat like pastiche, or, at its least successful, like parody, for the imagined literary quality of a writer and a text.

Imitation/intervention

Claims about the classic serial being 'faithful' to the novel, and to a 'spirit' that can be captured, are misleading given what separates the two, and, indeed, rather suspect in some ways.[24] They are, on the one hand, suggestive of the old myth that real art has a 'timeless quality' or 'essence' that stands indefinable and unquestionable, impervious to critical tradition, contemporary perspective and the politics of cultural value. On the other hand, they seem to obscure so much of the material nature of the classic serial. It is not that the films produced for 'mass' consumption do not, and cannot, come up to the standard of the 'great tradition' of novel writing, as so many have claimed, but, rather, that the notions of a classic serialization simply imitating or reproducing the novel, or capturing its 'essence', seem so critically naïve. There might be the illusion of a film 'bringing the novel to life', but actually classic serializations are specific cultural products operating under material circumstances that simply did not, and do not, apply to the novel. They are also interventions, more transformative than reproductive and certainly more active in sustaining and creating cultural meanings than might be thought.

One dimension of this intervention is the effect not just of sustaining the ideologized concept 'Literature', but of doing so in a particularly cleaned-up, anodyne and, again, nineteenth-century way. Like Anglo-Irish versions of Celtic texts or Victorian bowdlerizations of Shakespeare, television versions of the classic novel are invariably expurgated. The target, however, is no longer sexual content. In fact, this is often exaggerated or invented in modern styling, perhaps especially when Austen is the writer being televised. The makers of the 1972 *Emma*, for instance, felt so starved of sexual content that they invented a highly unlikely scene where Mr Elton straightens Harriet Smith's dress at the leg. In the 1995 *Pride and Prejudice* there is the entirely un-Austen-like image of Darcy (played by Colin Firth) taking an impromptu dive into a lake and emerging to drip suggestively at the feet of a startled Elizabeth Bennett. This, with its romantic and highly sexualized overtones, became a defining promotional shot for the production. More usually, then, it is perspectives, and narrative strategies, that now seem distorted, excessive or 'beyond reason', that disappear from television, rather than sex or 'bad' language. Thus, the televised Lawrence is a Lawrence without the fascism and romanticized as a class hero; Dickens is stripped of the dark excesses of his grotesquerie and the specifics of his social comment, which is presumably one reason why Fagin in *Oliver Twist* is traditionally softened from irredeemable otherness as a Jew into a more ambiguous trickster/magician figure and so on. This smoothing out of the novel tradition to produce a homogenized genre may also be reflected in the canon as it is has been interpreted by the BBC classic serial, by a 'Literature' configured primarily from notions of English 'realism' (Austen, Dickens, Eliot, Hardy and Lawrence) instead of from different traditions, represented by such figures as, say, Rabelais, Sterne, Woolf, Richardson, Joyce and Beckett.

Further dimensions of this intervention have already been suggested in this essay. It seems quite clear that a British corporation constructing 'Literature' in terms of English writers and idealized notions of English identity, to be sold worldwide as an English product, must surely work in fairly conservative ways. Indeed, it is possible to argue that the BBC and the classic serial fight something of a rearguard action in this respect. Whereas the traditional literary canon has been seriously scrutinized and interrogated in other institutional contexts – libraries, schools, publishing houses and, perhaps especially, university departments – television, at least as represented by the classic serial, has managed to maintain a literary tradition that is predominantly white, English and male. Austen remains the essential exception that confirms the latter hegemony, although her status in terms of the classic serial far exceeds any role of token female writer.

The BBC has serialized the work of a great many 'classic' authors, including Balzac, the Brontes, Collins, Dickens, Dumas, Eliot, Hardy, Hemingway, James, Scott, Stevenson, Waugh, Wells and Zola, but there is a sense in which the Austen novel remains pre-eminent as a subject for classic serialization, a fact explained by Monica Lauritzen in terms of economics and conservative cultural politics. 'For a television audience of family viewers, *Emma* is...perfect in the eyes of those responsible for the program output. It is limited in scope (and thus quite cheap to film) and safely traditional in its outlook.'[25] The effect of this identification between Austen and safe pleasure is worth comment. The development of Austen as the author most frequently visited and revisited by modern television, as Lauritzen implies, has meant rather more than the production of entertaining spectacles of historical recreation. In yet a further example of what Alison Light and others have understood as the 'conservative modern',[26] the Austen serial has commercialized a strong conservative domain in a contemporary and technological context. Conservative sexual identities, for example, (the remote, authoritative male, the English rose, the gamine and so on) are reproduced and maintained in the Austen serial. Traditional class systems are configured as the essential social structures, and traditional authority is upheld. The landed elite, for instance, is defended in this environment, sometimes reformed by the better elements of the bourgeoisie and invariably associated with essential 'English' qualities romanticized as universals. Urban life is marginalized, indeed, in its most radical form it is excoriated as an invention quite alien to the native English intelligence. Perhaps above all, the Austen novel has become a springboard for that elevation of pragmatism and fair play into 'the English way'. Silent about radical change and social conflict, the Austen novel, updated as an electronic and digitized culture, becomes the means by which a timeless order is managed and maintained as 'England'. It is hardly surprising that this package sells and achieves such substantial commercial backing from the corporate world.

Notes

1. John Ellis suggests that American film-makers relied less on the classics than on popular literature, whereas in Britain the reverse was so. There may be some room for doubt here, however. Gainsborough films, for instance, which had a considerable influence on classic serials, worked a great deal with popular novels. See 'The Literary Adaptation', *Screen*, 1982, vol. 23, p. 3 and Len Platt, *Aristocracies of Fiction: The Idea of Aristocracy in Late-Nineteenth and Early Twentieth Century Literary Culture* (Westport CT: Greenwood, 2001), pp. 139–41.
2. See Siegfried Kracauer, *The Nature of Film: The Redemption of Reality* (London: 1961), p. 217.
3. See Asa Briggs, *The History of Broadcasting in the United Kingdom* (Oxford: Oxford University Press, 1965), vol. 2, p. 169.
4. Paul Kerr, 'Classic Serials – To Be Continued' in *Screen*, 1982, vol. 23, p. 15.
5. See Monica Lauritzen, *Jane Austen's Emma on Television: A Study of a BBC Classic Serial* (Gotenborg: Gotenborg Studies in English, 48, 1981), pp. 9–11.
6. See Kerr, 'Classic Serials', p. 18.
7. Kerr argues that the classic serial is 'an embodiment of British television', p. 6.
8. George W. Brandt, '*The Jewel in the Crown* – the Literary Serial; or the Art of Adaptation' in George W. Brandt (ed.), *British Television Drama in the 1980s* (Cambridge: Cambridge University Press, 1983), p. 198.
9. This, of course, is the classic, Reithian expression of the BBC mission.
10. See Raymond Williams's account of 'Literature' in *Marxism and Literature* (Oxford: Oxford University Press, 1977), pp. 45–54.
11. Jonathan Miller in the James McTaggart lecture given at the Edinburgh International Festival (1983). Quoted in Brandt (ed.), 'The Jewel in the Crown', p. 196.
12. See Lauritzen, *Emma on Television*, p.11.
13. Brandt, for instance, believes that culture 'has always extended itself in the retelling and remaking of narratives.' It is this general approval that underpins his championing of *The Jewel in the Crown* series. He is dismissive of criticisms about the Anglo-centric nature of this production. See Brandt, '*The Jewel in the Crown*', p. 197.
14. See Sue Birtwistle and Susie Conklin, *The Making of Pride and Prejudice* (Harmondsworth: Penguin/BBC, 1995).
15. This was Colin McCabe's position, at least in regard of film versions of the novel generally. See 'Realism and the Cinema': Notes on Some Brechtian Theses', *Screen*, 1974, vol. 15, pp. 7–27. For an account of critical responses to his argument, see Kerr, 'Classic Serials', pp. 10–11.
16. '[W]hat is the justification of spending money if you're just going to produce a series of pictures alongside the dialogue of the novel? You have to offer an interpretation.' Andrew Davies reported in Birtwistle and Conklin, *The Making of Pride and Prejudice*, p. 3.

17. Birtwistle and Conklin, *The Making of Pride and Prejudice*, pp. 32 and 42.

18. See Ellis, 'The Literary Adaptation', p. 3.

19. Daniel Bell, *The Cultural Contradictions of Capitalism* (London: Heinemann, 1976), p. 105ff.

20. 'The principle of Hollywood Aristotelianism...[means that] all elements of the film – spectacle, diction, character and certainly thought – must be subordinated to plot, the prime arbiter.' George Bluestone, *Novels into Film* (Berkeley and Los Angeles, 1968), p. 103.

21. Birtwistle and Conklin, *The Making of Pride and Prejudice*, p. 13.

22. Andrew Davies reported in Birtwistle and Conklin, *The Making of Pride and Prejudice*, p. 13.

23. Quoted in Lauritzen, *Emma on Television*, p. 47.

24. '[W]e always thought it was important to go for the spirit of the original book', Sue Birtwistle quoted in Birtwistle and Conklin, *The Making of Pride and Prejudice*, p. viii.

25. Lauritzen, *Emma on Television*, p. 49.

26. Light's account of a modernism that is conservative focuses on the English novel between the wars. See *Forever England: Femininity, Literature and Conservatism Between the Wars* (London and New York: Routledge, 1991), pp. 14–19 and pp. 61–112. For an account of the conservative modern in late-Victorian and Edwardian musical theatre, see Len Platt, Musical Comedy on the West End Stage, 1890–1930 (Palgrave-Macmillan, 2004).

ASPECTS OF THE SOAP OPERA AND OTHER STORIES

Dorothy Hobson

The soap opera and continuous series are major forms of drama production which dominate national and global television. An understanding of the phenomena of the soap opera necessitates grounding it as a part of broadcasting. It is its role within the broadcasting industry and its relationship with other broadcasting forms which accounts for its unique relationship between its producers and its audiences.

The soap opera is a form which is revered by fans, reviled by some critics. Its history spans and reflects social change, artistic and cultural development and national and international broadcasting history. For broadcasters, the soap opera could be seen as the perfect television form: it achieves and retains audiences, gains press coverage, creates controversy, brings in advertising revenue, supports a public service ethos and generates discussion, dissection, analysis and astonishment at its survival and evolution (Hobson 2003: xii).

At a simple level, the soap opera is a radio or television drama in series form. It has a core set of characters and locations and is transmitted more than three times a week for fifty-two weeks a year. The main focus of the narrative is on the everyday personal and emotional lives of its characters. Secondary characters come and go. The drama creates the illusion that life continues in the fictional world even when viewers are not watching. The narrative progresses in a linear form through peaks and troughs of action and emotion. It is a continuous form with recurrent catastasis as its dominant narrative structure. It is based on fictional realism and explores and celebrates the domestic, personal and everyday in all its guises. It works because the audience has intimate familiarity with the characters and their lives. Through its characters the soap opera must connect with the experience of its audience, and its content must be stories of the ordinary (Hobson 2003: 28).

The soap opera and literary theory

While soap opera is studied in relation to television theory and theories of audience it is, in fact, to literature and literary theory that we can look also for close theoretical relationships. Established as a modern form of drama it is possible to see the soap opera as having its origins in oral literature, folk tale, storytelling. The soap opera embraces the traditions of drama and the novel, including the serial form popularized in the nineteenth century and the dominant theme of the soap opera is fictional realism which again relates the form to the literary realists of the eighteenth and nineteenth centuries. From Richardson's *Clarissa*, through the nineteenth-century serials of Charles Dickens, the domestic and personal detail in the novels of Jane Austen and George Eliot, the tales of northern life written by Mrs Gaskell to the modern literature of Barbara Pym, all tell tales and stories of the everyday lives, loves, joys and sorrow of the characters. The essence of these literary works feed into the essence of soap operas because the main credentials of their central and peripheral characters is that they are totally believable and their lives are full of incidents and emotions which are universal (Hobson 2003: 28).

Popular cultural forms, whether literary or television texts, have always attracted criticism. Indeed the criticism which was levelled against the novels of the eighteenth century and the realist novels of the nineteenth century was that they were about the everyday lives of ordinary people. When the nineteenth-century realists wrote about their own works they could have been writing in defence of the twentieth- and twenty-first-century soap opera. In the early nineteenth century, when the new literary form of the novel developed in Britain, the works of Defoe, Richardson and Fielding instituted a break from the existing literary traditions which had taken romance, fantasy and the epic as the dominant form. Watt (1972) describes the novel with its concentration on the individual:

> The novel is the form of literature which most fully reflects this individualist and innovating reorientation. Previous literary forms had reflected the general tendency of their cultures to make conformity to traditional practice the major test of truth; the plots of classical and renaissance epic, for example, were based on past history or fable. This literary traditionalism was first and most fully challenged by the novel, whose primary criterion was truth to individual experience – individual experience which is always unique and therefore new. (Watt 1972: 13)

The novel was, in effect, new; it broke from literary traditions. What the writers Defoe and Richardson did was develop and use different forms to tell the stories of their protagonists. Traditional plots were rejected and individual human experience and the way that individuals coped with their lives became the subject of the novel. According to Watt, when Defoe began to write his fiction he did not follow traditional plots but 'allowed his narrative order to flow spontaneously from his own sense of what his protagonist might plausibly do next' (Watt 1972: 14).

What developed from this perspective was that the individual experience was important – a break from the previous belief that 'universals' were of paramount importance. This is one of the main connections between the literary genre of the novel and the radio and television form of the soap opera.

The relationship between individual and universal experience is crucial in relation to the appeal of the soap opera. However, what has now developed in the form of the soap opera is that the experiences of the individual are seen as valuable precisely because they *do* carry resonance with universal experiences. The individual is appreciated because they share experiences, feelings and emotions with the audience. While it is not seen as a pure literary form, soap opera can be seen as developing directly from the novel.

And one of the main connections is through the vital importance of characters to carry the narrative and to bring universal stories to the audience.

In this chapter, I will explore the relationship of the soap opera to some further aspects of literary theory and identify literary theoretical perspectives which can be applied to the television genre. Among the concepts, which are considered, are Forster's *flat and round characters*, which can be used to explain the strength of the characters in soap operas. The concept of the *Bildungsroman* is applied to the development of young characters who have grown up within the soap operas over the last twenty years and their relationship to the social conditions which have prevailed makes them an example of the *Bildungsroman* within the television form. And the theory of readership, which Kendall L. Walton designated as the audience 'pretending belief', is easily applied to explain the engaged relationship of the soap opera audience to the form. Finally, the narrative of the continuous series is defined in relation to literary theory, when I discuss and develop the concept of what I term *recurrent catastasis* to explain one of the mechanisms of narrative which ensures the continuing appeal of the genre for its audience.

Forster's theories of the novel and the soap opera

The most important part of any soap opera is its characters. Characters are created by writers, augmented by the choice of actor made by the director, and finally brought to life by the actor who brings their own interpretation and something of themselves to the character. I intend to use Forster's thesis on the novel (Forster 1971) and apply some of his criticism to an analysis of the soap opera. Forster sees 'story' as the most important element within the novel, which is also the view of some soap producers; others, including the author, believe that characters are the most important element within the soap opera. Forster defines story as 'a narrative of events arranged in a time sequence' (Forster 1971: 38) and tells us that once we know the story, 'we need not ask what happened next, but who did it happen to?' (Forster 1971: 51). The crucial questions to ask about any soap opera are who are the characters and what is going to happen to them? Forster was writing at a time when only movies were available and before the growth of the television soap opera, but some of his observations on the difference between the novel and the drama are relevant to the later development of the genre of the soap opera. He identifies that while characters in novels are works of art, and the barrier of art divides them from us, nevertheless, he continues, they are 'real not because they are like ourselves (though they may be like us) but because they are convincing.' (Forster 1971: 69) One of the major appeals of the soap opera is its characters, and one of the debates which surround the popularity of the genre is the question of why is this so. Forster's thesis that characters are 'real' because they are convincing offers one answer to the popularity of the characters in soap operas. While he states that they are not popular because they are like us, that is not, in fact, the full argument in relation to characters in soap operas. Soap opera characters are believable because they are both convincing and their behaviour is either like ours or recognizable as behaviour which we see from our friends, family or acquaintances. Characters must carry the verisimilitude of the series by creating the relationship with the audience which they recognize and with which they acquiesce. Audiences must feel that the way that the characters behave is believable. This does not mean that they can never act 'out of character' for this would mean that there could be no character development, but that their behaviour is such that the audience will say, 'Oh, yes, I can see why she has done that now. It's because of x,y,z'. Characters must be constant but with the ability to 'surprise'. That is what makes them human and in Forster's term – round characters.

A further important element in Forster's thesis is his identification of and differentiation between his 'flat and round' characters. This too is beneficial when analysing the appeal and strength of the characters in soap operas. Each is important in the success of the soap opera. Forster believes that flat characters are important because they are easily recognized whenever they come in 'recognised by the reader's emotional eye'. He also sees them as important in that they are unchanging and provide a permanence in literature. Forster believes that flat or two-dimensional characters are not as big achievements as round characters, nevertheless, they play an important role in both the novel and dramatic forms. Forster relates his flat characters to the seventeenth-century humours or types of characters which were easily recognizable and perform specific functions in literature. Soap operas also have their own flat characters, who never have a major role and rarely have a major storyline. Sometimes they are there to aid major characters in their own stories but while some have a short stay, others remain at the level of supporting characters in the series. The idea of a flat character, representing certain characteristics can also be applied to characters when they are first introduced into a soap opera. Characters in soap operas can be criticized for being stereotypical, but I have argued (Hobson 2003: 83) that this is not the case because most characters are in soap operas for a long period and, while they may be introduced for certain characteristics, they do develop and reveal that they are, indeed, round characters. While characters in novels may remain 'flat' as they have only one purpose to serve, the majority of characters in soap operas, because of the long-running nature of the form, develop and evolve and become 'round' characters. For the most part, if they do not become round characters they are written out of the series.

When Forster introduced his concept of flat and round characters he identified the element which creates the main appeal for the novel. Forster indicates that the novelist reveals what s/he wants to about characters. and the reader can know what the novelists want them to understand,

> But people in a novel can be understood completely by the reader, If the novelist wishes; their inner as well as their outer life can be exposed. And this is why they often seem more definite than characters in history, or even our own friends; we have been told all about them that can be told; even if they are imperfect or unreal they do not contain any secrets, whereas our friends do and must, mutual secrecy being one of the conditions of life upon this globe (Forster 1971: 55)

One of the ways to explore the concept of the round character in soap opera is to see them in relation to their ongoing role within the series. Many of the characters in soap operas are so well established that they appear as if they would exist outside the series. Their characteristics combined with the acting and personal attributes of the actors and actresses portraying them are established over years of appearing in series, and this has the effect of creating characters who appear as if they would exist outside the series. Indeed, it is because the characters from soap operas are portraying 'ordinary' people that they have the effect of appearing so 'real'. They give the impression that they could be moved from one series to another across the genre.

In the same way that some of the strongest characters in novels have a presence which appears to exist outside the novel, so some of the soap opera characters have the ability to appear as if they could exist outside their own fictional setting.

Bildungsroman – growing up in soap operas

Bildungsroman is a term which is applied to novels which show the growth and development of a young character. Often inexperienced, foolish and innocent, the characters in such novels show how they grow and develop through their lives, with the help and sometimes hindrance of their family and friends. They also interact with the social conditions of the period of their stories and reflect the sociological impact of their surroundings on their lives. This concept of the *Bildungsroman* is one which can easily be applied to the soap opera. Children and young people have a major function in soap operas and whereas they did not always have roles which progressed through the series, since the advent of *EastEnders* and more recently in *Coronation Street*, there are characters who have begun as young children and who have had major storylines which have progressed through their lives. In *EastEnders* the teenage characters who were in the series at its inception in 1985 have now grown to be adults. The audience has watched the characters and shared their experiences. Ian Beale, Sharon Watts and Martin Fowler whose own conception was part of the early storylines of *EastEnders*, reflect the age of the programme and their life experiences have progressed with the sociological changes which have happened during the 22 years of their life.

Entering the series as a young man, the longest serving British soap opera character, Ken Barlow in *Coronation Street*, was a newly qualified teacher when the series began in 1960, and he has progressed through 47 years and shown representations of issues of class, sex and age in innumerable storylines. When the series began in the 1960s the first group of post-Second World War, working-class university graduates were emerging from university and taking their first job. Ken Barlow was representative of the first generation of young people who had been educated and who had to cope with the cultural changes which had happened to his self-perception and his perception of his family and their working-class cultural norms. He returned from college where he had been training to become a teacher and was rather ashamed of his mother's low-level job working in a hotel kitchen, although his feelings about the job were as much about the fact that she went out to work at all as it was about the nature of her job. The class conflict was intensified by the father who challenged Ken's freedom to take a new girlfriend out for a drink in the hotel where his mother worked, and his father compounded his control of the house and his right to uphold his working-class values when he worked on the puncture of the bike of his younger son in the kitchen. This mortified Ken who saw it as a terrible rejection of his newly acquired social values. Ken has progressed through innumerable life experiences both personal and professional with many romances, marriages, divorces, fatherhood with varying degrees of success, change of jobs from teacher to journalist, to retired supermarket worker who dabbled in local history and local newspaper feature writing. His life has embraced changes in cultural and sociological norms, and he functions as a commentator and, sometimes, victim of the changing fortunes with which he has had to cope.

Some of the characters who began as babies in the series have grown up in the dramas and their lives have reflected the times during which they have lived. An example is a storyline which has developed over the last seven years incorporating the elements of *Bildungsroman* in that it tells the story of a young girl and some of the vagaries of life with which she has had to cope in her teenage years. The character, Sarah Louise Platt in the Granada Television soap opera *Coronation Street*, has told the story of a young teenage girl who becomes pregnant at age 13. The character has been in the programme since her birth and the audience have watched her grow and seen her life, which has been quite traumatic since her birth, again reflecting social issues and contemporary values. Her conception was itself the subject of a dramatic storyline when her mother, Gail, had had an affair with the Australian cousin of her husband, and the identity of the baby's father was in dispute. When it was found that Gail's husband, Brian, was the father of the baby, he returned to the marital home, but when Sarah Louise was two years old he was stabbed to death leaving a nightclub. When Gail remarried the younger Martin Platt, he became Sarah Louise's father and she grew up with her older and younger brother as part of the new family. When the new storyline was revealed it brought into the series a story which told the audience of an experience which, unlike most soap opera stories, was outside their own everyday lives. While teenage pregnancies are more common, a pregnant 13-year-old is rarer. A very young teenage pregnancy affects the whole family, but especially the young girl for whom it will change the rest of her life. The realization that you are pregnant is either a cause for absolute joy or absolute despair, dependent upon any number of variables in your life. Perhaps the worst scenario is when the mother-to-be is herself a child. The build up to the revelation of the pregnancy was handled by intimations of Sarah Louise having an eating disorder and when her mother took her to consult her doctor the audience expected a story handling this issue. Instead, Sarah Louise is as shocked as her mother to learn that she is pregnant. Each element of the storyline is then handled to give the necessary information for the family to proceed. Sarah Louise admits that she has once slept with a boy in her class and as a result she is pregnant at 13.

The storyline reflected the various cultural norms and changing values which were prevalent at the time. Sarah Louise's mother reacted with her own characteristic anger and accusations, while her grandmother Audrey reminded her daughter that she had been an unmarried mother when she had been pregnant with Gail over forty years ago, albeit not at such a young age. The reactions of various members of the community revealed understanding, empathy and compassion, prejudice and condemnation. The experience of the pregnancy, childbirth, looking after a young baby and the subsequent years of constant childcare has shown the difficulties that early motherhood can bring, and at each stage of her life Sarah Louise has shown that her own life and the life of her daughter, Bethany, are inextricably linked. Storylines in other soap operas, *Crossroads* in the 1970s and *Emmerdale Farm* in 1989, had young unmarried girls becoming pregnant, but these babies did not become part of the series. In the first instance the mother married and the child was taken to America by his new father and in the second the character moved to Scotland with her newly born daughter. It could be said that this was to reflect the social mores which were not quite united on the attitude to teenage pregnancy. By 2000, the acceptance of teenage pregnancy was more part of the cultural and social norm and although it would cause comment and discussion within the community, the series felt able to include the storyline and not lose the empathy of their viewers.

The repercussions of the event have continued and when Sarah Louise became involved with a young neighbour, Todd, he sacrificed going to Oxford University to stay with Sarah Louise and Bethany. Since the outcome for soap opera stories is rarely one of a happy ending, it should not have been surprising that the production continued Sarah Louise's story with an unhappy event. When she became involved with Todd she thought that she might be moving to a more settled romantic and domestic element in her life. However, the intertwining story of the romance of the two characters continued the elements of *Bildungsroman* within the soap opera. While Sarah Louise believed that Todd is committed to a life with her, Bethany and the new baby they were expecting, Todd had his own life challenges to cope with via a new element in his storyline. In a previous incident he had kissed Sarah Louise's brother, Nick, who was outraged and accused him of being gay and tried to break up the relationship. Todd refused to confront his own feelings and when Sarah was pregnant he readily agreed to marry her and was thrilled at the prospect of becoming a father. But in a dramatic twist, Todd meets

Karl, a charismatic gay nurse and their mutual attraction results in them beginning a sexual relationship and in Todd feeling that he must confront his own sexuality and confessing his relationship with Karl to Sarah Louise. The ensuing dramatic situations enabled every character who has any connection with Todd and Sarah Louise to express their opinions, prejudices and personal fears about one young man's sexuality and its effect on others. Every prejudice and contemporary fear and positive attitude is expressed by the characters in the series. This form of drama is an example of the power of the soap opera to provide public service broadcasting as the various views are examined by different characters and then are discussed by the audience as they react with their own views on the situation. However, in terms of literary theories, this is another example of how the soap opera has become a contemporary vehicle for the *Bildungsroman*, and the story of Todd and his awakening to his sexuality is expressed in a way that is culturally and historically specific. *Coronation Street* is set in Manchester, which has a thriving commercial sector with bars, nightclubs, restaurants which are specifically, though not exclusively, used by gay young men and women. Canal Street was made famous outside Manchester when it was the location for one of the most exciting television dramas about Manchester's gay community, *Queer as Folk*, which brought the area to the notice of viewers of the series. In the story of Todd's awakening realization of his sexuality, which *Coronation Street* portrayed, the production used Canal Street as a cultural reference and location for Todd and Sarah Louise and other young characters in the soap to go on a night out. Filming in actual locations, the series showed the celebratory and yet ordinary nature of the 'night out' and only Todd had difficulty in coping with the sexual tensions which he was experiencing.

Emotional and practical realism set in a specific cultural and historical moment is a major part of soap opera and the inclusion of this storyline gave both a sense of drama and the continuation of the *Bildungsroman* of a number of the characters. The ability to develop the stories of young characters is an ideal concept for the soap opera; because of its continuous nature it means that they can grow up in the series and not only develop as characters but respond to and reflect changing mores of cultural and sociological norms to provide a commentary on changing contemporary values.

Playing with the form

One of the major criticisms which is made of the soap opera viewer is that they are incapable of distinguishing between fiction and reality. Whereas audience studies, Brown M. E. (1987), Buckingham (1987), Gillespie (1995), Hobson (1982, 1987, 1990, 2003, 2004), reveal that audiences have an active relationship with the form and engage with the characters and their stories in a way which indicates that they are 'believing' the fiction in as much as they are ready to interpret and question or cohere with the series. However, the most pertinent and sophisticated theory which explores the phenomena of reader/viewer and the cultural form with which they engage is Walton's theory of 'pretending belief'. The notion of 'pretending belief' (Walton in Furst 1992: 221), the unpacking of the intimate relation between the real world and fiction ones (232) is elegantly expounded by Kendall L. Walton. This exposition of the relationship of readers to the world of fiction and the emotional involvement with the characters and their lives is applicable to an understanding of the relationship of audiences to serial fiction. The belief in the fictional creation of a soap opera rests on the assumption on the part of the audience that the action continues to take place while the cameras are not watching the programme. The crucial element necessary for the acceptance of the genre is that the audience does believe, albeit in a 'pretending' or 'playful' (Walton in 1992: 223–4) relationship with the fiction, that life goes on when they are not watching. Walton's concept of the awareness of the reader of fictions: 'Human beings make up stories and tell them to each other. They also listen, entranced, to stories which they know are made up' (Walton 1992: 218) rests on the connection between the world of fiction and the real world as a psychological interaction. He asserts:

> We feel a psychological bond to fictions, an intimacy with them, of a kind which normally we feel only toward things we take to be actual (Walton1992: 223–4).

His exposition on the way that audiences relate to fiction in a playfully engaged manner is pertinent to explaining and understanding how audiences engage with events in soap opera and share their playfulness with other members of the audience, even when they may be strangers. Whilst disbelief may have been suspended in order to first engage with the fiction, the interplay of audience with drama requires an intellectual and psychological re-engagement to take the events performed in the soap opera and to talk about them in relation both to the characters in the drama and their relationship to real events of which the audience has experience. 'Playing' with the fiction and the characters and then taking the concepts and characters and eventsfrom the fiction to discuss them with friends and colleagues is both a form of playing, in that they acknowledge that they are engaging with a fictional form and also using the fiction in a creative way as they tell their own versions of the stories. This concept of play is particularly apposite when considering the ways that soap opera viewers approach the genre. They will happily discuss storylines in their everyday conversation mixing comments about characters in the series with comments about their own friends and family. One comment came from four pensioners travelling on the inter-city train from Birmingham to London who spoke about their various family members and their respective grandchildren and then moved immediately into a conversation involving Emily and Arthur and whether he was a con man and she would suffer in the end. The Emily and Arthur in question were characters in *Coronation Street*, and their speculation about the characters was a playful inclusion of the fiction into the reality of their own lives (Hobson 1982: 125). Similarly, students talking in a supermarket talked of their friends and then moved on to asking what each thought about Grant Mitchell character in *EastEnders* and whether he had really been drowned or 'done a Harold'.

Harold was a character in *Neighbours* who disappeared into the sea and was thought to be drowned, only to turn up many years later suffering from amnesia. The conversation moved between the two soap operas, the two characters and their potentially related actions, without ever indicating that they were talking about a soap opera (Hobson 2003: 4). This is clearly not an example of confused audience members but an example of audiences playing with the fiction. Thinking of the relation of audiences to soap opera and using Walton's theory gives a new perspective on the audience relationship with the genre.

Recurrent catastasis – the narrative engine of the soap opera

This essay has taken literary theory and applied it to the soap opera. The final section takes literary terms and creates a new way of describing the engine which drives the narrative. Unlike other literary and television genres, the soap opera does not need to have an ending. Forster wrote that 'nearly all novels are feeble at the end. This is because the plot requires to be wound up' (Forster 1971: 102). In the novel there is a requirement for symmetry and resolution. Soap opera has a dramatic structure which is a continuous form; there is no need to round everything off because the series continues. Constructed as a continuous series, each episode has a climax or 'hook' at the end to bring audiences back the next week for the next instalment. However, storylines must reach their climax and periodically individual storylines reach a form of resolution. While a resolution may be appropriate for individual stories as the soap opera or drama series continues daily, weekly, monthly, yearly and decade after decade the multiple storylines continue. What is unique about the soap opera is that the dramatic engine which drives the narrative along is what I would term *recurrent catastasis*. Catastasis is 'the part of a drama in which the action has reached its height' (Chambers 1972: 201). In the soap opera genre, as one dramatic narrative theme reaches its climax, another one is developing, working towards its own climax. The audience never needs to be disappointed because there is always another climax coming along, and this means that there is always a reason for the audience to stay watching. After one storyline is complete, there is always a continuing story to bring the audience back to the next episode. The climaxes continue and the *recurrent catastases* drive the drama of the soap opera. This is more than the simple notion of the dramatic ending to an episode; it is a vital ingredient in the narrative structure of the soap opera which differentiates it from other serial forms. It is the multi-layering of plots and climaxes which gives the form one of its major attractions for audiences. The *recurrent catastases* mean that each climax can be followed by another one and the audience continue to be attracted to the stories with ongoing pleasures of resolutions and anticipation of further resolutions to follow.

Literature and the soap opera

The similarities between the soap opera and literary forms are many, and this chapter has only been able to indicate a few of the connections and ways in which literary theory can be used in analysis of the televisual genre. The importance of character, the playful engagement by audiences with the characters and their stories, the thematic concepts of fictional and societal development as explored in the *Bildungsroman* and the narrative engine which drives the series all have literary connotations which can be applied to the soap opera. While fiction explores and tries to understand and explain the human condition, particularly through the novel, so the soap opera takes the universal issues which affect the human condition and explores these through the vehicle of their characters and their stories. The genres are close and using literary theories which have been developed to explain the more respected literary forms can help to explain the popularity and universal appeal of the soap opera.

References

Brown, M. E. (ed.), 1990: *Television and Women's Culture*. London: Sage.

Buckingham, D., 1987: *Public Secrets: EastEnders and Its Audience*. London: British Film Institute.

Chambers, W & R., 1972: *Chambers Twentieth Century Dictionary*

Gillespie, M., 1995: *Television, Ethnicity and Cultural Change*. London: Routledge.

Forster, E. M., 1971: Aspects of the Novel. Harmondsworth: Pelican.

Hobson, D. 1982: *Crossroads: The Drama of a Soap Opera*. London: Methuen.

——, 1989: Soap Operas at Work. In Seiter, E., Borchers, H., Kreutzner, G., and Warth, E. (eds), *Remote Control : Television Audiences and Cultural Power*. London: Routledge.

——, 1990: Women Audiences and the Workplace. In Brown, M. E., (ed). *Television and Women's Culture*. London: Sage.

——, 2003: *Soap Opera*. Cambridge: Polity.

——, 2004: Everyday People, Everyday Life. British Teenagers, Soap Opera and Reality TV, in Feilitzen von, C. *Young People, Soap Operas and Reality TV*. Nordicom, Goteborg University, Sweden.

Walton, K. L., 1992: Pretending Belief. In Furst, L., *Realism*. London: Longman.

Watt, I., 1972 (1957): *The Rise of the Novel: Studies in Defoe, Richardson and Fielding*. Harmondsworth: Pelican.

SHAKESPEARE ON AMERICAN TELEVISION AND THE SPECIAL RELATIONSHIP BETWEEN THE UK & THE USA

Curtis Breight

The Tudors, especially Henry VIII (1509–1547) and Elizabeth I (1558–1603), were the first English monarchs to recognize the centrality of navies to empire building. They laid the foundations for a later British Empire whose reliance upon sea power is matched by that of today's American Empire. US Naval power underpins what Chalmers Johnson has recently termed an 'empire of bases', which features at minimum 'some 725 bases in thirty-eight countries' (154). But until the recent ascendancy of the so-called 'Neo-Conservatives', who in the first few years of the twenty-first century have formulated US foreign policy predicated on seemingly new strategies such as pre-emptive war, there has been a traditional reluctance to conceive of the United States, at least in public discourse, as an empire. Instead, what Christopher Hitchens has viewed as a kind of passing of the imperial torch from the UK to the USA is typically euphemized in political discourse as a 'Special Relationship' between Britain and America. Although one might wish to attribute this relationship to the 'founding' of America through English colonization in the early seventeenth century, there is no natural or obvious reason why origins should guarantee such a close and ongoing alliance beginning in the twentieth century. After all, the American Revolution was a bloody and lengthy struggle against British rule, and the War of 1812 even featured British troops burning the American Capitol. Although 'empire' itself is a concept and practice with which many are uncomfortable (to say the least), I would submit that empire is the ongoing reality that is difficult to perceive because it is a shared, Anglo-American Empire, existing under the political nomenclature of Special Relationship. And one key figure, William Shakespeare, serves in the capacity of cultural unifier and differentiator for this imperial amalgamation.

Empire, as evinced by a historical succession of failed empires, is difficult to construct, manage and maintain. Conversely, it is easier to run an empire through partnership(s). Although there are different schools of thought regarding what constitutes the Special Relationship – or even whether or not there is a Special Relationship at all – the key factor that underpins Britain and America as what Kathleen Burk calls 'permanent allies' (Burk, 254) is war. Winston Churchill is generally regarded as the first statesman to coin the phrase 'Special Relationship', and he did so 'as a means of advancing British security interests, namely by convincing a reluctant United States to become involved in war and cold war on Britain's side' (Hahn, 276). The 'heart' of the Special Relationship lies in 'defence and intelligence cooperation, but the relationship extended also to foreign policy' (Dumbrell, 8). Moreover, since England came to rely upon America to help finance its twentieth-century wars (Burk, 243–260), it is crucial to acknowledge the extent to which the UK and the USA are economically intertwined. Even today, each country is the number one investor in the other's economy. Militarism, surveillance and hard economics underlie what the 'functionalist' view of the relationship perceives as 'shared interests' as opposed to 'sentiment and shared culture' (Dumbrell, 9). According to John Dumbrell, 'during the Cold War...the UK enjoyed privileged access to nuclear information from the United States. This, along with the intimate intermeshing of US and British intelligence under the UKUSA agreement of 1947, formed the essence and beating heart of the Cold War "special relationship"' (124). The reality of militarism as the foundation of the Special Relationship is that despite the end of the Cold War, the USA has been able to count on the UK as its main ally in both Gulf War I and Gulf War II.

On the other hand, according to Dumbrell, 'shared history, culture and language do count for something' (9): 'Those British diplomats who sought to promote the specialness of the London-Washington axis had to start somewhere. They started precisely from culture and sentiment' (10). And where better to start than with the single most important cultural figure in the English language? According to Lawrence Levine, whereas Shakespearean drama was a fixture of nineteenth-century American popular culture, Shakespeare's works gradually disappeared from the popular realm and were relocated in elite culture (1–9 and 11–81). Although one might wish to qualify Levine's argument by citing the extensive reproduction of Shakespeare in silent film beginning around the outset of the twentieth century (see Ball; Uricchio and Pearson, chapter 3), his relative disappearance from the popular stage seems not to be coincidental with the rise of American Empire, which can more or less be dated to 1898, when the USA finished off the Spanish Empire in places such as Cuba and the Philippines. Shakespeare, I hypothesize, was co-opted by elite culture because of world views shared between British and American elites that made the real decisions about empire. The primary poet of one empire became the primary poet of another, or more precisely, Shakespeare became the cultural linchpin for the budding Special Relationship that needed to mask empire due to titular considerations of 'democracy'.

The promotion of Shakespeare from popular to elite culture coincides with the social juncture at which the Anglo-oriented identity of the USA was seemingly threatened by an influx of non-western European immigrants (Dumbrell, 4). In an important, recent book entitled *Imperial Brotherhood: Gender and the Making of Cold War Foreign Policy*, Robert Dean documents how 'an old-stock WASP upper class' engineered social differentiation and restriction of privilege through new institutions:

> The publication of the first *Social Register* (1888), the foundation of the first country clubs (1882), the social dominance of the fraternal clubs and secret societies at Harvard, Yale and Princeton, and the emergence of a network of exclusive metropolitan men's clubs represented one aspect of old-stock patrician efforts to create and maintain class solidarity in the face of threatening new developments (18).

Perhaps most crucially, the educational apparatus for young members of the elite became the prime intersection at which American and British culture joined together:

> The American boarding school, modeled more or less explicitly upon the British public school, trained the adolescent sons of a moneyed elite in the stoic virtues of manliness and service to the state. An 'invented tradition', this culture helped to create, reproduce and validate a self-conscious ruling class. Animated by fears of the corrupting influence of the city with its immigrant hordes, Anglophile patrician old-stock Americans patronized the newly founded or recently reconfigured boarding schools in New England, such as Groton, St. Paul's, Choate, Phillips Exeter and Andover and others (Dean, 18).

In the television film discussed below (*My Dark Lady*), a British Shakespearean actor facilitates the escape of an adolescent black boy from an inner-city ghetto to a rural boarding school, 'Essex', that clearly replicates the New England schools listed by Dean. The Englishman is able to accomplish this feat by training his young charge and the boy's prostitute mother in various types of upper-class refinement, especially Shakespeare. It is, of course, ironic that the escape benefits an African American boy whose predecessors at Essex would have been the sons of white parents who feared the prospect of 'race suicide' (Dean, 19), but the basic cultural implication is obvious: one escapes from the mean streets of America and into the system through Anglophile maneuvers such as intellectual subordination to the superiority of Shakespeare.

As Burk explains, "British power has been peculiarly dependent on financial power" (244). But once Britain had been brought to its economic knees by the necessity of borrowing from America to finance its two twentieth-century world wars, the economic status of the USA and the UK was suddenly reversed. Almost overnight, at the end of World War II, the USA became the predominant military and economic power while the British Empire lay in ruins. The UK thus needed the Special Relationship far more than the USA did, so the question became – what could the UK contribute to such a relationship? Certainly Britain was in a position to offer bases to the American military, which are always considerably valuable, but I would argue that the UK was more broadly situated to proffer a kind of cultural cachet to an America that was perceived – and perceived itself – as culturally inferior. One can discern the process of cultural exchange by considering that Americanization of Britain is largely economic and takes place at a popular level. The USA wishes to export films, music, sports, fast food and other products mostly associated with low culture. On the other hand, the UK and, significantly, US anglophiles tend to anglicize America primarily by exporting the best of English high culture. As D. L. LeMahieu observes, 'if in [American] schools and universities, courses in British history suffered from diminishing enrollments, visual depictions of the British past enjoyed wide appeal', with the following implications:

> Some have claimed that...costume dramas reinforced an ideology of social and political conservatism. Class and hierarchy...so permeated these productions that they became a celebration of the class system. Powerful evidence supports this contention. Again and again, the dress, manners, politics, cultural taste and social prejudices of a privileged elite attract detailed, loving attention. Artfully photographed scenes luxuriate in conspicuous consumption: the imposing country house, the manicured lawn, the deer park, elegant aristocrats at a glittering occasion. If some critics accused these dramas of nostalgia, the compensatory emotion of a declining power, others indicated how they reinforced orientalist assumptions, even and perhaps especially when claiming to challenge the imperial legacy (261).

A mere glance at representative British cultural products indicates an emphasis on high culture and/or intellectualism. British (or British-oriented) cinema in America is characterized by period adaptations or modernizations of canonical English authors such as Jane Austen, Charles Dickens, E. M. Forster and William Makepeace Thackeray. British television for the USA is a bit more diverse, featuring comedy as well as high drama, but ironically and appropriately enough, it largely appears on the public broadcasting network (PBS) that is associated with high culture. The cable channel 'A&E' ('Arts and Entertainment') televises the British series *MI-5*, whose representation of the British domestic intelligence service raises no eyebrows among American audiences. Despite the fact that the USA also nurtures special relationships with Israel and Mexico, it is doubtful if either of these countries could export a series on their intelligence services without people wondering about the suitability of such programming for American television. But it is specifically Shakespeare that is the touchstone of the Special Relationship on the cultural level of both cinema and television. The last decade and a half has witnessed an explosion of Shakespeare on the big screen, from traditional costume dramas such as Kenneth Branagh's *Henry V* (1989) to teen-oriented modernizations such as *Scotland, PA* (2002). But even domestically produced American TV programs such as *One Tree Hill*, a high school basketball drama first aired in the fall of 2003, is framed in its pilot episode by the acceptable intellectualism of its lower-class, street ball hero, Lucas Scott. Near the outset of the episode Luke is reading John Steinbeck's *The Winter of Our Discontent*, a novel whose title is drawn from the opening line of Shakespeare's *Richard III*. And at the end of the episode Luke quotes Shakespeare's *Julius Caesar* in voice-over, drawing a parallel between his challenge to his upper-class half-brother and Brutus' decision to roll the battlefield dice at Philippi

("There is a tide in the affairs of men", 4.3.217ff.). Perhaps most tellingly, in a kind of fantasy episode of *JAG* (Judge Advocate General), naval legal officers are entrusted with protecting a First Folio of Shakespeare's complete works. I cannot imagine a more symbolic gesture toward the Special Relationship than that between a US Navy steeped in tradition – as navies tend to be – and the foremost author of British culture.

When I was beginning to rewrite the previous paragraph, I happened to take a break in order to watch the American late-night comedy show, *Saturday Night Live* (23 October 2004), hosted by Jude Law. Law, whose own career includes playing the central role in an adaptation of the Thomas Hardy novel *Jude the Obscure*, appeared in a spoof of the *Masterpiece Theatre* series, in this case *Jane Eyre*. While the actress playing Jane is cast as bookish and plain, Law plays a horny protagonist who repeatedly tells Jane not to go upstairs, where he is constantly meeting a clearly American nymphomaniac who only wants to have sex and eat fast food. As Levine claims in order to prove his assertion about the popularity of Shakespeare in nineteenth-century American culture, it is impossible to parody what people do not recognize (4, 15). According to Timothy Brennan, "Masterpiece Theatre is a cultural colonization in the heart of empire, an attempt to fuse together the apparently incompatible national myths of England and the United States in order to strengthen imperial attitudes in an era of European and North American decline" (374). Fortuitously, the *Saturday Night Live* skit helps to substantiate my argument that British culture is typically equated in America with high culture. The episode also contained a skit featuring a press conference involving President George Bush and Prime Minister Tony Blair (played by Law), probably occasioned by contemporaneous news headlines announcing the transfer of nearly a thousand British combat troops from the relatively pacified region of southern Iraq to the hotspot of Baghdad. The question-and-answer session with the 'press' detailed that Blair's popularity had plummeted after this announcement, whereas Bush's remained steady regardless of how the war was perceived to be going. The clear implication was that the American public is simply stupid, and in a telling moment, even Law could not refrain from raising an eyebrow. The Special Relationship is fundamentally predicated on the notion that American brawn requires British brains, as the skit's distinction between an acute Blair and a moronic Bush so heavily suggests.

Although Shakespeare is now most closely associated with cinema, especially given the rapid rise of the auteur Kenneth Branagh, it is television that helps to secure audiences for Shakespeare on the big screen, at least in the USA. It is not simply the case that American television is dominated by cable and satellite programming, whose wealth of movie channels guarantees that most Shakespearean cinema will eventually appear on the small screen; but also that television Shakespeare functions to prepare spectators to value cinematic Shakespeare. The latter, however, is typically marked by trends. For example, the current period starting around 1989 appears to wish to attract popular audiences given the teen-oriented productions such as *10 Things I Hate About You* (1999) and *O* (2001); modernizations such as *Richard III* (1995) and *Titus* (2000); and even Branagh's *Henry V* (1989) which was intended for the *Batman* audience (see

Breight, 108). The era of the Vietnam War featured productions such as Orson Welles' *Chimes at Midnight* (1965) and Roman Polanski's *Macbeth* (1971), both of which take a dim view of high political power. Indeed, this era corresponds with a temporary breakdown in the Special Relationship occasioned by Britain's refusal to provide any troops to support the American-led war (Dumbrell, 147–159). Thus, it is interesting to ponder the fact that the next major explosion of filmed Shakespeare occurs on television in the aftermath of the war. The BBC complete works of Shakespeare, broadcast on American public television between 1978 and 1985, epitomize how the Special Relationship works across presumably discrete areas of interest. The BBC project, conceived about the same time (1975) as Senator Frank Church's commission was investigating intelligence-oriented abuses by organizations such as the CIA, is not simply a cultural or educational phenomenon. Major American corporations underwrote a good percentage of the series' financing. Most of the productions were traditional, emphasizing language over action or experimentation (see Willis, chapter 1). Thus, although this series was not suitable for a mass audience, it was clearly intended to educate a segment of the American population in a different way by providing all of Shakespeare. It is not hard to imagine that one reason for undertaking such an ambitious project was the desire to help repair the fractured Special Relationship by emphasizing Britain's unique cultural role in that relationship. It is a case of Shakespeare usefully made to enter, "once more unto the breach" (*Henry V*, 3.1.1).

Sometimes it seems justified to ascribe cultural significance to an otherwise obscure film because it addresses how Shakespeare on television can function to deepen the Special Relationship at its most fundamental level of education. In the 'Not Rated', made-for-cable-television movie entitled *My Dark Lady* (1986), an over-the-hill English Shakespearean actor named Sam Booth is forced to take refuge in a black inner-city neighborhood in Buffalo, NY after committing an impromptu crime. Booth had been auditioning for the role of Santa Claus in a television commercial for Babinski's Department Store, whose ludicrous theme of 'Christmas in July' featuring a bikini-clad blonde sitting on Santa's lap suggests the level to which Booth has fallen. The store's owner, Horace Babinski, epitomizes the 'ugly American'. He is loud, rude and overbearing. When a fellow actor interrupts the end of Booth's first take, asking Babinski how long he must wait to audition since he has another audition elsewhere, Babinski dismisses the actor through sarcastic mockery, asserting that he wouldn't want to get in the way of his career with something 'so mundane as a paid TV commercial'. Babinski's overly harsh dismissal of the actor makes Booth respond by quitting his audition, and he does so by distinguishing between himself and Babinski, between being an 'actor' and a 'clown'. Moreover, he demonstrates the difference between himself and Babinski by adapting part of Shakespeare's most withering insult (delivered by Kent to Oswald in *King Lear*, 2.2.13–20):

> You, as the immortal bard would say, are nothing but a knave, an eater of broken meats, a proud, shallow, worsted-stocking, lily-livered whoreson, and nothing but the composition of a beggar, coward, panderer, and the son and heir of a mongrel bitch.

Babinski knows that he has been insulted, but he fails to comprehend the meaning of the insult. Meanwhile Booth storms off the set and begins to fill his sack with items from the store.

The idea of American cultural inferiority is not only established by Babinski's failure of comprehension, but also suggested by two forms of seemingly gratuitous physical disability. Babinski has a cast on his right arm, made all the more prominent by metal screws, and a young male shopper wearing a knee-to-foot cast and hobbling on crutches is knocked over during a chase sequence in which Booth accomplishes his getaway. Indeed, the entire opening of the film features Booth using his wits to evade and/or deceive Babinski and his employees, his landlady, the police and a little boy whose bicycle he expropriates after promising a new one for Christmas. Although the film clearly marks itself as comedy through these sequences, there is also an implied antagonism between England and America in that Booth makes fools out of his pursuers. The film literally announces cultural difference from the very outset, when Babinski's response to Booth's first take is that he should try it again, 'this time in American'. After dismissing the other actor, Babinski orders his crew to get back to 'merry old England here'. Babinski's public relations employee explains to Booth that they need to please Babinski's 'people' given that it's a television commercial, 'not Shakespeare at the Old Vic'. Here television is placed in opposition to Shakespeare, as though they were antithetical. Television is common, associated with the 'people', whereas Shakespeare is exclusive. Television, in fact, recurs in this film as something inferior or as a form of unreality.

If *My Dark Lady* initially announces itself as comedy with a serious undertone, the generic markers are complicated when Booth rents a room from a 34-year-old black widow, Lorna Dahomey, who is prostituting herself in the hopes of raising enough money to send her 11-year-old son Malcolm to boarding school. Lorna's husband, whose photograph in military uniform appears on a mantel, had died 'in the service' when Lorna was 23, which suggests that he died near the end of the Vietnam War. Lorna is determined to save her son from a comparably threatening life in the ghetto, where Booth's first visual encounter is with a young black drug dealer later arrested by the police. But prostitution alone is not enough to facilitate escape. Perhaps predictably, Shakespeare becomes the instrument whereby Booth saves both Lorna and Malcolm. Booth seeks to dispose of a Santa Claus hat and broken sword by surreptitiously placing them in a garbage can, but Malcolm turns up unexpectedly and begins to ask questions. Booth's response is an attempt to deceive the boy by literally putting on a show, in this case a rendition of the dagger speech from *Macbeth* (2.1.33ff.). A neighborhood audience even gathers and applauds the performance. Booth then attempts to hide his costume in Lorna's attic, yet Malcolm follows and inquires about learning the speech. But first he asks Booth about the TV programmes on which he has presumably appeared, since this is a reasonable presupposition about actors. Booth retorts, "I've never been on the accursed tube, and never will. TV doth make midgets of us all. How can one compress the grandeur of all that was Shakespeare into a box that's two feet wide?"

After Booth judges that Malcolm is too young to learn Shakespeare, the boy begins to declaim the *Macbeth* speech from memory, substituting a few simpler expressions and using some ungrammatical street language. Nonetheless, Booth is amazed at Malcolm's talent and agrees to teach the boy. Booth's decision fits in with Lorna's plans for Malcolm. If television renders people 'midgets', Shakespeare ennobles them. Lorna is worried that Malcolm (who already knows about the prostitution) will discover his mother's secret. She reveals to Booth that she knows about his crime and makes a deal with him about keeping their mutual secrets. Lorna plans to send her son to boarding school not just to maintain his presumed ignorance about her activities and get him away from a deleterious environment, but also to improve his chances for rising in an initially unspoken social class system:

> Malcolm's gonna have a chance to meet the right people....Malcolm's gonna have a head start in life, a real head start, not like the ones you hear about on TV.

Meeting the 'right people' constitutes reality to Lorna, whereas television propagates myths. The film's internal negative commentary on television is, of course, highly ironic in that television touting Shakespeare is the means by which the Malcolm-esque, after school, adolescent viewer can also rise in the system. But money is not enough, or rather, Lorna realizes that she too needs Booth to provide the high-class lessons so that she can go 'uptown' and make the large sum of cash requisite for boarding school tuition.

Booth, however, is initially reluctant to help Lorna because he has his own career problems. An offer from a theater in Seattle to play the second gravedigger in *Hamlet* and a couple tiny parts in *King Lear* demoralizes rather than encourages Booth because he still believes himself capable of playing the role of Lear and playing it well. He even dons theatrical make-up and declaims part of the king's storm speech during an evening thunderstorm (3.2.1ff.). Significantly, Lorna's interruption of Booth's ranting speech, which she claims is 'interfering' with her John's 'pleasure', makes Booth almost seamlessly switch from the storm speech to Lear's encounter with Cordelia:

> I am a very foolish old man,
> Four score and upward, not an hour more nor less,
> And, to deal plainly,
> I fear I am not in my perfect mind. (4.7.60–63)

When Lorna first agreed to rent him the room, she had asked for references and Booth responded by giving her theatrical reviews. One of the better jokes in the film occurs when Lorna reads that Booth "played the king [Lear] as though someone else had played the ace." Thus, beyond being over-the-hill, Booth is a mediocre actor and a man whose sanity is being tried by a thwarted career.

Booth's decision to go to Seattle begins to change only when a new john physically abuses Lorna and Malcolm. Booth chases him down and fights him, sword against metal pipe, while quoting Shakespeare. Eventually the john flees, exclaiming that he won't fight 'no crazy man', but Lorna becomes anxious about Malcolm's possible response to the incident. If the initial relationship between Booth and the Dahomey household features the old actor's superiority as tutor to Malcolm, Lorna's 'proposition' that Booth also teach her is cast as a form of mutual support: "You've brought gifts into this house that can help us to get out....I'm askin' you to take what you got and what I got so we can all get out of here. Think of it as your starring role, real life." Booth's resistance to Lorna's proposal finally alters after learning that Malcolm comprehends the reality of his mother's 'boyfriends', and then witnessing the arrest of a young drug dealer across the street in tableau – complete with distraught mother.

Although Lorna's first foray into high society, a classy French restaurant, results in comic disaster, her next attempt is both successful and obliquely indicative of what underlies the Special Relationship. As the camera first closes in on a calendar with 'Defense Contractors Convention' penciled in, and then pans across a red, white and blue banner stating, 'Star Wars Are Our Wars', Booth's voice-over captures the essence of Reagan-era remilitarization:

> Lorna, the premier American bandit of yesterday once said he robbed banks because that's where the money is. Today, defence is where the money is, with contracts to pad and kickbacks to give. So to succeed here you have to take the offensive. Be bold, provocative, demanding. And, above all, don't be disarmed.

Although the sequence is clearly comedic, featuring a john who exclaims that he'll hire Lorna by putting her fee into 'next year's budget, under basic procurement', Booth's voice-over has a serious component. After defeat in Vietnam, there was a perceived need to become 'offensive' again and certainly not to disarm, which connotes disability. The success of Lorna and Booth thus symbolizes good prospects for renewed success in the Anglo-American alliance.

Their next attempt to raise money together occurs at an educators' masked ball, where Lorna first has an unsuccessful encounter with the man who runs the school that Malcolm will soon attend, Headmaster Park. But after this failure, a man in a skeleton costume (Samuel Macmillian) spirits Lorna away to his mansion, where he tries to commit suicide. Lorna stops him, and when he tries to dismiss her by saying that someone in her position could not possibly understand how the loss of his wife and daughter to a drunk driver has devastated his life, Lorna replies by stressing that he has a son who needs him. They have an exchange highlighted by Lorna's application of Shakespeare to his situation, lines which she has learned from Booth (slightly adapted from *A Winter's Tale* and *The Merry Wives of Windsor*):

> Lor. What's gone and past help should also be past grief.
> Sam. What?
> Lor. 'Tis not good that children should know any wickedness. Old folks have discretion, as they say, and know the world.

Macmillian's reward of a thousand dollars is enough to help enable Lorna to pay for Malcolm's first semester tuition.

But 'parents' weekend' at Essex School is the occasion for Lorna's success seemingly to be dashed. Whereas Malcolm is thriving at sports and cast as the lead in *Othello*, Park recognizes Lorna and informs her that Malcolm must leave school at the end of the semester. Booth twice plots to blackmail Park by threatening to expose his association with a prostitute, but neither attempt works and a kind of *deus ex machina* in the form of Macmillian is required to resolve the dilemma. He arrives to address the alumni and there discovers Lorna, who accompanies him on stage while he speaks to the group and donates $500,000 to the school. Macmillian even hires Lorna, which suggests that she will accomplish her dream of giving Malcolm a real head start in life.

As for Booth, his life and career are also revitalized by the success of the Dahomeys, since the Seattle theater company sends him another letter offering the part of the first gravedigger in *Hamlet*, which is arguably a major role in any production of that play. Booth's announcement to Lorna regarding the renewal of his theatrical career takes place in front of a portrait that features an apparent family (mother, father and two children). Shots featuring portraits in the background are one of the few repeated cinematic devices of this film, and the framing of Booth in front of a family portrait would seem to suggest that he and Lorna have made Malcolm's life complete through mutual effort. Likewise, Lorna is framed in front of a portrait featuring a mother and her children at Macmillian's mansion, which indicates that she symbolically fills the maternal role by saving his life and restoring him to his son.

But in a film filled with portraits, including one of Malcolm X perhaps meant to suggest what Malcolm Dahomey could become under the 'wrong' tutelage, it is the photographic family-style portrait of Lorna, Malcolm and Booth that prevails by implying that people symbolizing America and England are unified. This photograph, taken in the midst of a sequence involving Booth's initial training of Malcolm in performance skills, is emblematic for a theory of narrative prosthesis drawn from the relatively new discourse of disability studies (see Mitchell and Snyder, 4–10). The disabled Babinski and the disabled male shopper of the film's opening sequences prepare us for a generalized American disability epitomized by Lorna's failure to secure her son's freedom from a dangerous environment. If she can only partially secure his freedom by lowering her stockings (as it were), she can complete this process through pulling herself up by Shakespearean bootstraps. Shakespeare, through Booth, is the prosthesis whereby Lorna's entrepreneurial American economic efforts are crucially enhanced by British cultural superiority. The special relationship of these characters is a microcosm of that larger Special Relationship that must be relentlessly renewed through hybridization of low and high cultures whose "boundaries...are constantly being blurred, challenged, and redrawn" (Strinati, 45).

Notes

1. Although I could not ascertain when *My Dark Lady* was initially broadcast on television, I first saw it on Starz! during late spring, 1995. Its programming slot confirms it is intended for a 'family' or, more specifically, a 'child' audience, and its tone aligns it with the 'after-school' special genre of made-for-TV movies in the USA.

2. At the conclusion of the credits to *My Dark Lady*, a mature child's voice-over introduces the next movie, *Jimmy Valentine*, by stating satirically, "Warning: 'Hang Time' on Starz! may contain programming unsuitable for your parents". The child's voice is 'ungendered', i.e. it could be an older yet pre-pre-pubescent boy or a teenage girl. But the key point is that the voice-over isolates the audience as privileged by their youth and the (supposed) inaccessibility of their programming to adult monitoring. It is, of course, ironic that a film such as *My Dark Lady* functions largely as paternalistic acculturation of ignorant yet exceptional youth.

References

Ball, Robert Hamilton, 1968: *Shakespeare on Silent Film: A Strange Eventful History*, New York: Theatre Arts Books.

Breight, Curtis, 1991: 'Branagh and the Prince, or a "royal fellowship of death"', *Critical Quarterly* 33.4, 95–111.

Brennan, Timothy, 1987: 'Masterpiece Theatre and the Uses of Tradition', in *American Media and Mass Culture: Left Perspectives*, ed. Donald Lazere, Berkeley: University of California Press, 373–383.

Burk, Kathleen, 2000: 'War and Anglo-American Financial Relations in the Twentieth Century', in *Anglo-American Attitudes: From Revolution to Partnership*, eds. Fred Leventhal and Roland Quinault, Aldershot, England: Ashgate, 243–260.

Dean, Robert, 2001: *Imperial Brotherhood: Gender and the Making of Cold War Foreign Policy*, Amherst: University of Massachusetts Press.

Dumbrell, John, 2001: *A Special Relationship: Anglo-American Relations in the Cold War and After*, Basingstoke, England: Macmillan.

Hahn, Peter, 2000: 'Discord or Accommodation? Britain and the United States in World Affairs, 1945–92', in *Anglo-American Attitudes: From Revolution to Partnership*, eds. Fred Leventhal and Roland Quinault, Aldershot, England: Ashgate, 276–293.

Hitchens, Christopher, 1990: *Blood, Class, and Nostalgia: Anglo-American Ironies*, New York: Farrar, Straus & Giroux.

Johnson, Chalmers, 2004: *The Sorrows of Empire: Militarism, Secrecy, and the End of the Republic*, New York: Metropolitan Books.

LeMaheiu, D. L., 2000: 'America and the Representation of British History in Film and Television', in *Anglo-American Attitudes: From Revolution to Partnership*, eds. Fred Leventhal and Roland Quinault, Aldershot, England: Ashgate, 261–275.

Mitchell, David, and Sharon Snyder, 2000: *Narrative Prosthesis: Disability and the Dependencies of Discourse*, Ann Arbor: The University of Michigan Press.

Shakespeare, William, 1994: *Four Tragedies: Hamlet, Othello, King Lear, Macbeth*, eds. T. J. B. Spencer, Kenneth Muir, and G. K. Hunter, London: Penguin.

Shakespeare, William, 1965: *Henry V*, ed. John Russell Brown, New York: Signet, 1965.

Shakespeare, William, 1963: *Julius Caesar*, eds. William and Barbara Rosen, New York: Signet.

Strinati, Dominic, 1995: *An Introduction to Theories of Popular Culture*, London and New York: Routledge.

Uricchio, William, and Roberta Pearson, 1993: *Reframing Culture: The Case of the Vitagraph Quality Films*, Princeton: Princeton University Press.

Willis, Susan, 1991: *The BBC Shakespeare Plays: Making the Televised Canon*, Chapel Hill and London: The University of North Carolina Press.

Television as History: History as Television

Anne Wales

> 'History now occupies a significant place in the most influential medium of popular culture – television. There are more history programmes than ever before, giving rise to the quip that history is the 'new gardening'.'[1]

In the revised introduction to the third edition of *The Pursuit of History*, John Tosh comments on the significance of history programming which is such that it would probably be true to argue that television is the means by which most people learn about history. However, this is not a new phenonmenon, as dating back to the 1960s and 70s there have been various types of television history including dramatization of actual events and people , such as Edward VII, Henry VIII's six wives, Elizabeth I, periodized fictional drama such as *Upstairs, Downstairs*, compilation documentaries drawing on archive footage, other visual sources, interviews and narration, such as *World at War* and programmes featuring academic historians such as A. J. P. Taylor or Michael Wood.

History programming developed during an era in which television 'provided the concentrated essence of a nationally authorised culture'.[2] Historical narratives continue to reflect themes of empire, nationhood, family and collective identities despite the trans-global nature of the medium. The proliferation of history programming in the 2000s, as identified by Tosh, has continued to include a focus on emperors, kings and queens, such as in Rome, Egypt, Charles II or Elizabeth. History continues to provide the backdrop for fictionalized drama, such as in *Foyle's War*, set in World War II, and historians such as Simon Schama and David Starkey continue to be media stars. New dimensions have been introduced, such as historical reality television in the form of programmes like *The 1900 House*, *The 1940 House* etc., and the constant availability of historical documentaries on satellite channels.[3] Historical television programmes seem to have the function of containing globalized trans-national communication within familiar stories of nation and community. It seems significant that 'history' contains the word 'story' and that in some languages the words for history and story are the same.[4] 'Historians are not after all only concerned to explain the past; they also seek to reconstruct it or recreate it'.[5]

The reflexivity of the medium of television and the discipline of history has been a focus of scholarship for the last thirty years. In the 1970s, Newcombe argued that 'a special sense of history' is one of the key characteristics of television programming.[6] A meeting of the Secretariat of the Prix Italia in 1980, including delegates from France, Britain and Italy, debated the role of television as object, source for and producer of history. One paper commented on television's emulation of cinema in the creation of history as spectacle, citing 1970s costume dramas. This observation highlights the need to distinguish between programmes about history and programmes which themselves constitute media events because of the way in which they raise historical awareness. Arthur Marwick noted the need to differentiate between television as a source for studying history and television as a means of communicating history.[7]

John E. O' Connor was one of the first historians to highlight television production and reception, as well as texts, as providing frameworks for historical inquiry. A decade later, drawing on scholarship in film history, he identified four frameworks for the historical analysis of film and television as being the moving image as representation of history, the moving image as representation for social and cultural history, actuality footage as evidence for historical fact and the history of the moving image as industry and art form.[8] During the 1990s, two special issues of the journal *Film and History* were devoted to the theme of 'Television as Historian'.[9] The introductory article identified television's relationship with history as having seven key characteristics:

- Television is the principal means by which people learn about history
- History on television is big business and, as such, is central to institutional histories of television
- The technical and stylistic characteristics of television influence the historical representations produced
- History lends itself to television because history has the ability to embody the concerns of the present
- Television history provides us with a useable past
- Television history as collective memory is the site of mediation where professional history meets popular history
- Television as a medium is capable of presenting the flipside of presenteeism – pastism.[10]

Challenges faced in defining television's relationship to history and historiographical critique include the almost ahistorical nature of Television Studies which has tended to organize itself with reference to media concepts such as genre, institution, text and audience. There are many introductory texts which include a chapter on television history.[11] There are a number of texts which could be described as engaging with historically evidenced social theory, some of which acknowledge the role of television in creating public history but which do not further the historiographical debate or engage with historical methods.[12] There are a number of broadcasting histories which create narrative histories of broadcast institutions, drawing on historical source materials such as policy documents, committee reports, memoirs, audience research and scheduling.[13] Problems associated with creating histories of television programmes themselves, including issues of access to early programmes and selective archival practices have been noted.[14] Added to this is television's ephemeral approach to its own history, with a focus either on broadcasting institutions or on memorable programmes.[15]

Debates about the role of television history within television studies have centred on the over-arching debate within Media Studies of Cultural Studies vs political economy leading to an inherently historical approach in areas such as revisionist approaches to writing about television news, the relationship between television and public events, institutional histories and some types of audience study.

Arguably, it is within feminist television criticism and race and ethnic studies that attempts have been made to produce a historically grounded approach to the television text – '...during the 1980s and 90s a focus on intertextuality, production conditions and the social history of texts, rather than close textual readings of programmes, became important to scholars looking at the social construction of woman'.[16] Developments in broadcasting in the 1980s and 90s produced a concern to cater for diversity. Within the academy, published work looked at issues of black representation and the experiences of black people working in the industry.[17]

However, it is scholarship in film studies on film history and film's role in screening public history[18] and developments in history such as social history, 'history from below', gender history and the new cultural history which have provided the academic underpinning for a genuinely historically grounded approach to the study of television and for a consideration of television as historian from the standpoint of historiographical critique.

The reciprocity of television and history has developed alongside the emergence of a critical historiography, emerging out of challenges to historical materialism with its meta-narratives and concern for causation and process, from the Annales School[19] and others concerned with collective identities and social memory and from postmodernism, 'the linguistic turn' in history and the new cultural history.[20]

Central both to the function of history on television and to the role of television within contemporary historiography is the notion of collective memory. Collective identity is reliant upon a shared interpretation of events, with social memory being handed down through narratives and rituals. One of the functions of television within social memory since the 1950s has been to create narratives and rituals through the televising of public events, with each occasion providing a model for the next similar event which would then be approached by a television audience with particular expectations which would be confirmed and challenged.

Samuel has argued that there are three recurrent features of social memory which are respect for tradition, nostalgia and progress.[21] One of the most mediated events of the late twentieth century was the funeral of Diana, Princess of Wales in 1997. The televised event both accorded with and departed from the narratives and rituals associated with state funerals. Tradition was reflected in the flag-draped coffin transported on a gun carriage and in the filming of the architectural features of Westminster Abbey. Aspects of the event such as Earl Spencer's speech and Elton John's rendition of 'Candle in the Wind' provided a sense of progress and hinted at the potential transformation of royalty. Experience is central to the creation of memory, with social memory being created through the meshing of representation and reality. Nostalgia was evoked through romanticizing the life of 'the people's princess' and through the sense of loss which was prevalent amongst those interviewed.[22] Diana's funeral was not only seen by television audiences but was simultaneously watched and experienced by crowds outside Westminster Abbey through outdoor television screens and speakers. Therefore, the event entered the domain of social memory both as a mediated public event and through what J. B. Thompson has termed 'the publicness of co-presence'.[23] The experience and emotions of those present outside Westminster Abbey became enmeshed with televisual representations of the event itself. Hence, social memory was created at the interface of media representation and individual experience which together forge a collective identity and history.

The centrality of television to social memory can be illustrated by the way in which people remember key events both in terms of televised images and with reference to their own personal lives. For example, most people can remember what they were doing when hearing of the sudden death of famous people such as John Lennon or Princess Diana and many of these associate the news with its television coverage. A notable feature of the Vietnam War was the way in which for the first time horrific war imagery entered people's living rooms, connecting everyday life to political events. Historically, the very occasion of public events has often been the pivotal factor in the acquisition of a television set, with ownership of television sets and size of audience increasing significantly in Britain in 1953 on the occasion of the coronation of Queen Elizabeth II and in America in 1957 on the occasion of the second inauguration of President Eisenhower. The latter was both an unprecedented television spectacle and a technological triumph due to the use of videotape.[24]

Therefore, social memory forms at the intersection of experience and representation, with television as one of the prime mediators of both. It could be argued that television as historian is a far more complex concept than regarding it as either object, source or producer of history or as representation, but rather it is a process which converts memory to history and, as such, forms part of the new historiography which has developed and which, therefore, needs to be included as part of television criticism.

Traditionally, television criticism has presented 'liveness' and 'immediacy' as being key determinants of television. Arguably, this could have led to the situation in which the historical function of television has existed almost as a separate body of scholarship to 'Television Studies' which whilst it may embrace a historical dimension, rarely engages with historical methodology. However, it is the very 'liveness' of television which gives it the power to create memory as a social rather than an individual phenomenon, rescripting memories to conform to existing historical narratives. Television is the facilitator of cultural memory on occasions of national remembrance, mourning or celebration. For example, news coverage of the thirtieth anniversary of the first moon landing in 1969 was presented in terms of both the landing as an historical event, with original television footage containing Neil Armstrong's memorable and much-quoted phrase, 'One small step for man, one giant leap for mankind', and in terms of contemporary American national identity.[25] Hence, the 'usable past'[26] of the moon-landing relates to the politics of the present through the re-presentation of historical narratives which encourage the audience to 'remember' America's relationship with the rest of the world in terms of achievement, whilst 'forgetting' other aspects of American politics. Citing Foucault, Hanke has argued that in the popular media people are 'shown not what they were, but what they must remember as having been'.[27]

Television coverage of the first Gulf War in 1991 and its subsequent re-creation in historical programming is a case in point. The programmes accord with Samuel's definition of social memory, reflecting tradition through the scripting of narratives around key protagonists representing 'good' allied to contemporary western nationalism (Gorbachev, Major, Bush, Mitterrand and the US General Norman Swarkopfz, christened ' Stormin' Norman') versus 'evil' represented by Saddam Hussein. Nostalgia was evoked through the use of historical narratives in which Saddam was likened to Hitler and in which there were references to Roosevelt's 1942 interpretation of the United Nations. The technologically advanced weaponry of the 'clean war' represented the progress of western modernity and the torched oil wells of Kuwait symbolized a narrative history structured around oil and international law.[28] Thus, the social memory of the Gulf War presented in news and documentary forms selectively remembered the power of western nationalism to defeat an enemy likened to Hitler, whilst creatively forgetting issues relating to the future of the Arab states, the impact of the war on the Iraqi people and the cultural identities of viewers of the programmes. The latter was highlighted in an episode of *The Media Show* which showed Arab viewers in Britain discussing western news coverage of the war.[29]

At its best, television can provide socially relevant history able to provide a perspective on the present or the future. Some types of history demand a reflexive relationship between past and present and a subjective or intersubjective positioning within that history. Television programmes through their appeal to the emotions can achieve both these in terms of producing history as the re-creation of the past in the present. However, as Tosh has pointed out, the use of television as a historical source through the use of news coverage or in programmes broadcast during or only a few years following a set of events, provides the same dilemmas as the historian's traditional reliance on the press as evidence. Arguably, those who create programmes are concerned with good television before good history.[30] In this case, it has been argued that television is a primary source for how events were represented, not for the history of the events themselves.[31]

The observation that live media events compete with history writing in defining collective memory,[32] could be extended to all television programming. The 'pastness' of fictional television reveals a self-reflexive consciousness of history. For example, soap operas such as *Emmerdale* and *Coronation St* present us with a nostalgic vision of a community life which never existed, but which becomes our 'memory' of the past. Programmes such as *Heartbeat* draw on cultural texts of the past such as popular music and fashion. There have been a number of examples of historical programmes which in themselves have become 'media events' in terms of their roles within public discourse. For example, the German docu-drama *Holocaust* (1978) had such an impact it was described as a 'media event'.[33] In part, this was due to educational preparation.[34] This in itself demonstrates the role of television as educator and historian. In 1976 the documentary series *World at War* had engaged British viewers in the history of World War II from hitherto neglected perspectives. Drawing on a range of sources, it demonstrated the similarity between the broadcaster and the historian, both of whom interpret and select from sources and weave them into narratives.[35]

The historical reception of Alain Resnais' film *Nuit et Brouillard*[36] illustrates the impact of the moving image on historical understanding and within the processes of remembering and forgetting. Originally, the film was criticized for its denial of French involvement in the Holocaust and of Jewish people as the key victims. However, by the 1970s, visual understanding was such that the yellow star of David was seen to symbolize Jewishness.[37] In May 1990, following attacks on Jewish cemeteries in Paris, all five French national television channels postponed their schedules to broadcast *Nuit et Brouillard*, which was used subsequently within the French national school curriculum.

O' Connor has argued that the programme and book *Roots* (1976) exemplifies how the media of publishing and television can distort the academic practice of history.[38] Nonetheless, the television programme *Roots* played a role in raising awareness of the history of slavery. Fictionalized characters and dramatized events did not undermine the general historical information conveyed regarding the conditions of slavery. However, the issue is the extent to which television programmes simply create a new historical imaginary based on cultural capital formed around notions of nation and community rather than conducting evidence-based historical inquiry. Pierre Sorlin has argued that such programmes appeal to the emotions through visual impact rather than by inviting the viewer to argue or reason. 'Successful series like *World at War* have exposed the public to an unfamiliar type of history – visual history designed to strike by its evidence and through immediate contact, instead of convincing through reason or deduction.'[39] By contrast, John E O'Connor argues for the visuality of history, citing the moving image not only as having a role as public historian, but also as providing an important source of evidence – ' Imagine trying to do justice to the historical analysis of the Nazis and their propaganda machine by reading the manuscripts alone.'[40] Furthermore, television is intrinsic to the historical study of politics and culture since the 1950s. There have been instances in which television has almost created the events. The issue is that visual sources, like written ones, need to be approached by an external critique of the document.[41]

These debates point to the fact that historical television programming and the academic study of history on television draw on disciplines outside of film, television and media studies. There is a clearly defined system of historical knowledge from which television programmes take their material.[42] Therefore, there is a need both to establish the relationship of television to critical historiography and to take account of this within television studies and within television programme-making.

Similarities between media practitioners and professional historians and the importance of television to contemporary history have been noted.[43] Televisual history, like history writing, involves a tension between re-creating the past, in a way with which contemporary viewers (readers) can identify, and analysing and interpreting it. Documentary programmes such as *The Gulf War* provided over-arching meta-narratives based on western imperialism identified as the United Nations. From a historiographical point of view this approach, drawn from historical materialism, has been problematized as meta-narratives do not enable access to historical experience. However, critical historiography which has facilitated this through methodologies emerging through postmodernism and 'the linguistic turn' in history, such as understanding historical events as a form of discourse or in terms of the subjectivities of the historical actors, brings with it its own problems. Television, as a quintessentially postmodern medium, has been particularly effective in producing programmes which engage the viewer in historical experience at a subjective level. Dramatized reconstructions present the past from the standpoint of the historical actors. Contemporary viewers identify with the events and emotions from the standpoint of their own subjectivities and experiences which to some extent become universalized. Hence, the scene in *Roots* which evoked the most resonance and which is the one most broadcast as representative of the series as a whole was the one in which an enslaved family is separated, with a daughter being sold as a result of a minor transgression. The series as a whole provided a sequential narrative in which one could trace the history of those sold into slavery in Africa, and then experiencing the notorious Middle Passage[44] and subsequent integration into both white American society and the cultures engendered by the enslaved population of the Americas. Black viewers identified with *Roots* in terms of their 'own' black history. All viewers could connect with the universal notion of separation and loss. However, seeing history from the point of view of its key players, does not in itself lead to historical understanding. As John Tosh has pointed out, historical actors do not understand historical processes and '(r)ejecting all meta-narratives cannot make sense because narratives and meta-narratives are the kinds of stories that make action in the world possible.'[45]

The 1990s television adaptation of the novel *A Respectable Trade* enabled British viewers to engage with the tangled emotions of the victims and perpetrators of the slave trade as the programmes highlighted the social class dimension and the fact that all of those involved in the trade did not remain disconnected from those they had enslaved. In terms of a critique founded in the new historiography, the programmes can be seen as both serving the postmodern historical agenda and as providing some explanation of causation and process. The programmes represented different subject positions within the slave trade and examined the hierarchies of power created by race, gender and class. However, they also provided some explanation of how and why ordinary British trading families became involved in slavery. Television programmes need to be understood not only in terms of how they represent or create history, but also in terms of processes within broadcasting history and of television as the object of historical study. Historical programming and the creation of history through televisual representation's role in social memory can be understood to some extent within a wider social, political and academic agenda including the influence of Marxist and Feminist thought, the notion of 'history from below', the development of social history and gender history, the influence of the women's movement, the large body of scholarship on film history and the emergence of the new critical historiography. However, the *World at War* was not merely to address the need for audiences to appreciate different perspectives but for these to be contained within the meta-narrative of western imperialism, but also to enable ITV to compete more effectively with the BBC's output in current affairs and history programming. *Roots* was an attempt by ABC to engage with an emerging black television audience in a way which would appeal to a still predominantly white audience. *A Respectable Trade* was one of the products of the 1990 Broadcasting Act and its concern for 'quality, diversity and choice'.

Therefore, the way forward for television history and the basis for its critique would be to draw on debates in critical historiography which have emerged since the 1970s, striking a balance between the concern for causation and process of historical materialism, the concern for collective identities and 'total history' of the Annales School and others and the challenges of postmodernism, the 'linguistic turn' and gender history. History on television needs to develop both a diachronic and synchronic relationship to its subject matter, moving from a dramatic recreation of the past to include an explanation of historical process and an overlaying of historical issues onto contemporary ones, thereby appealing to viewers not only as emotional but also as intellectual and political beings. Television history and its criticism need to have a self-reflexive understanding of intertextuality. How does the television text which represents history, itself become yet another cultural artefact? How do television texts relate to other historical sources? The lessons of postmodernism have taught us that history writing like any other literary genre is constructed according to rhetorical strategies in which 'history becomes a parade of signifiers masquerading as a collection of facts'.[46] The same could be said of some television programmes.

A critical methodology for the analysis of such programmes would need to emerge from three key perspectives including an aesthetic approach in which the television text is seen as a form of history writing, a social historical approach in which the processes by which the programmes form part of social memory are evaluated and an institutional approach in which history programming is defined by, contributes to or contradicts developments in broadcasting. Methodological engagement with the two paradigms of the meta-narrative which takes into account causality and process within history, and intertextuality in terms of interpretation of sources, would effect a practice of history which would shape television as public historian, rather than television as heritage.

History programmes and programmes which enter social memory and become history need to be constructed and understood in terms of historical processes of causation; the relationships between historical texts, broadcasting institutions and the politics of production; and history as social memory which achieves political action or understanding in the present. Television criticism needs to acknowledge the role of television in history and to embrace methodologies based on historiographical critique, historical method and history writing.

Notes

1. Tosh, J., (2002): *The Pursuit of History: Aims, Methods and New Directions in the Study of Modern History*, London: Longman, revised 3rd ed., pp. xiv-xv.
2. Smith, A., (1998): *Television: An International History*, Oxford University Press, 2nd ed., p. 1.
3. *The 1900 House*, Channel 4 2000, and *The 1940s House*, Channel 4 2001, were documentary series in which a modern-day family lived in a house for a week in conditions as they would have been in 1900 and the 1940s respectively.
4. Tosh, J., op. cit. p. 141.
5. Tosh, J., op. cit. p. 175.
6. Newcomb, H., (1974): *TV: The Most Popular Art* New York: Anchor, p. 258–9.
7. Radio Televisione Italia, (1980): Report of Meeting Organised by the Secretariat of the Prix Italia held in Riva del Garda on 11–12 September 1980.
8. John E. O'Connor was co-founding editor of the Journal, *Film and History*. See O'Connor, J. E., (1983): *American History/American Television: Interpreting the Video Past*, Ungar and O'Connor, J. E. (1990) *Image as Artifact: The Historical Analysis of Film and Television*, FL: Krieger.
9. *Film and History*, (2000): Special Issue: Television as Historian, vol. 30: 1, vol. 30: 2.
10. Edgerton, G., (2000): 'Television as Historian: An Introduction' in *Film and History*, vol. 30: 1 (March).
11. Examples include Bignell, J., (2004): *An Introduction to Television Studies*, London: Routledge. Branston, G. & Lusted, J. (eds) (1998) *The Television Studies Book*, London; Arnold. Corner, J.

(1999) *Critical Ideas in Television Studies*, Oxford: Clarendon. Kaplan, E. A. (ed.) (1983) *Regarding Television: Critical Approaches: An Anthology*. Los Angeles: American Film Institute.

12. Examples include Ang, I., (1996): *Living Room Wars: Rethinking Media Audiences for a Postmodern World*, London: Routledge and Scannell, P. (1996) *Radio, Television and Modern Life*, Oxford: Blackwell.

13. Examples include Briggs, A., (1965–1979): *The History of Broadcasting in the United Kingdom*, vols 1–4, Oxford: Oxford University Press, Curran, J. & Seaton, J. *Power Without Responsibility*, Goodwin, A. & Whannel, G. *Understanding Television*, Hilmes, M. (2003) *The Television History Book*, London: BFI, Paterson, R. *A Suitable Schedule for the Family* and Scannell, P. *Public Service Broadcasting: The History of a Concept*.

14. Bignell, J., (2004): 'Television Histories' in *Introduction to Television Studies*, London: Routledge, p. 38.

15. Caughie, J., (2000): *Television Drama: Realism, Modernism and British Culture*, Oxford: Oxford University Press. Cited in Bignell, J. op. cit., p. 39.

16. Brunson, C., D'Acci, J., Spigel, L., (1997): *Feminist Television Criticism: A Reader*, Oxford: Oxford University Press, pp. 10–11.

17. Examples include Daniels, T., (1994): 'Programmes for Black Audiences in the Hood', S. (ed.) *Behind the Screens: The Structure of British Television in the Nineties*, London: Lawrence & Wishart, Hartman, P. & Husband, C. (ed.) (1975) *Racism and the Mass Media*, London: Davis-Poynter, Husband, C. (1975) *White Media and Black Britain*, London: Arrow Books, Pines, J. (ed.) (1992) *Black and white in Colour*, London: British Film Institute, Ross, K. (1996) *Black and White Media: Black Images in Popular Film and Television*, Cambridge: Polity Press.

18. For examples of scholarship on film and history, see Allen, R. C & Gomery, D. (1985): *Film History, Theory and Practice*, A. Knopf, Cames, M. (1995) *Past Imperfect: History According to the Movies*, Elsaesser, T. (1986) 'The New Film History', *Sight and Sound*, 55: 4, Grindon, L. (1994) *Shadows of the Past: Studies in Historical Fiction Film*, Temple University Press, Kuhn, A. & Stacey, J. (1998) *Screen Histories: A Screen Reader*, Clarendon Press, Mellencamp, P. & Rosen, P. (eds) (1984) *Cinema Histories : Cinema Practices*, American Film Institute, Nowell-Smith, G. (1990) 'On History and the Cinema', *Screen* 31: 2, O'Connor, J. (1990) op. cit., Rosenstone, R. (1995) *Revisioning History: Film and the Construction of a New Past*, Princeton University Press, Smith, P. (ed.) (1976) *The Historian and Film*, Cambridge University Press, Sorlin, P. (1980) *The Film in History: Restaging the Past*, Oxford: Blackwell.

19. The Annales School was a group of historians working in the early twentieth century who linked history to perspectives in the social sciences.

20. For examples of discussion on historiography in the 1980s and 90s, see Bann, S. (1990) *The Inventions of History*, MUP, Braudel, F. (1980) *On History*, Weidenfeld and Nicolson, Burke, P. (1991) *New Perspectives on Historical Writing*, Polity, Burke, P. (1995) *History and Social Theory*, Polity, Burke, P. (1997) *Varieties of Cultural History*, Polity, Evans, R. (1997) *In Defence of History*, Granta, Hobsbawm, E. (1998) On History, Abacus, Hunt, L. (ed.) (1989) *The New Cultural History*, California University Press, Jenkins, K. (1997) *The Postmodern History Reader*, Routledge, Jenkins, K. (1991) *Re-Thinking History*, Routledge, Le Goff, J. & Nora, P. (eds) (1985) *Constructing the Past: Essays in Historical Methodology*, Cambridge University Press, Marwick, A. (1989) *The Nature of History*, Macmillan, Shoemaker, R. & Vincent, M. (eds) (1998) *Gender and History in Western Europe*, Arnold, Southgate, B. (1996) *History:*

What and Why, Routledge, White, H. (1973) *Meta History and the Historical Imagination in 19c Europe,* Johns Hopkins University Press, White, H. (1978) *Tropes of Discourse: Essays in Cultural Criticism*, Johns Hopkins University Press.

21. Samuel, R., (1994): *Theatres of Memory. Vol 1: Past and Present in Contemporary Culture*, London: Verso. For further discussion of the relationship between history and collective memory, see Fentress, J. & Wickham, C. (1992) *Social Memory*, Oxford: Blackwell and Samuel, R. & Thompson, P. (1990) *The Myths We Live By* London: Routledge.

22. The Funeral of Diana, Princess of Wales, BBC 1, September 1997, 'The Week the World Stood Still', ITV, September 1997, The Mourning, BBC, December 1997.

23. Thompson, J. B., (1995): *The Media and Modernity: A Social Theory of the Media*, Polity.

24. Taves, B., (1990): 'The History Channel and the Challenge of Historical Programming' in *Film and History* vol. 30: 2.

25. *News at Eleven*, ITV, 16 July 1999.

26. Edgerton, G. 'Television as Historian: An Introduction' in *Film and History* vol. 30: 1 p. 7.

27. Hanke, R., (1990): '*Quantum Leap*: The Postmodern challenge of Television as History' in *Film and History* vol. 30: 2 p. 42.

28. Tosh, J. op. cit., p. 23, 'Critical Eye: Reasons for the Gulf War', (1991) C4, *The Gulf War*, (1991) BBC 1.

29. *The Media Show: The Gulf War*, (1991) C4.

30. Tosh, J. op. cit.

31. Radio Televisione Italia, (1980): *Report of a Meeting of the Prix Italia* op. cit.

32. Dyan, D. and Katz, E., (1992): *Media Events: The Live Broadcasting of History*, Harvard University Press. For further discussion, see Sobchak, V. (1996) *The Persistence of History: Cinema, Television and the Modern Event*, London: Routledge.

33. O'Connor, J., op. cit.

34. Radio Televisione Italia, (1980): *Report of a Meeting of the Prix Italia* op. cit., p. 193.

35. *World at War*, pr. Isaacs, J., (1974): Thames Television.

36. *Nuit et Brouillard*, (1955) : dir. Alain Resnais.

37. Rice, L., (1990): 'The Voice of Silence: Alain Resnais' 'Night and Fog' and collective memory in post-Holocaust France 1944–1974' in *Film and History* vol. 30: 1, pp. 22–9.

38. O'Connor, J., op. cit.

39. Sorlin, P., (1980): *The Film in History: Restaging the Past*, Oxford, Blackwell.

40. O'Connor, J. op. cit.

41. Ibid.

42. Ibid.

43. Radio Televisione Italia, (1980): *Report of a Meeting of the Prix Italia*, op. cit.

44. The Middle Passage was the route across the Atlantic used to transport the enslaved from Africa to the Americas via Europe.

45. Appleby, J., Hunt, L., Jacob, M., (1994): *Telling the Truth About History*, Norton p. 236. Cited in Tosh, J. op. cit., p. 197, footnote 52.

46. Samuel, R., (1994): op. cit.

'The story you are about to see is true': Dragnet, Film Noir and Postwar Realism

R. Barton Palmer

Conceived by radio actor Jack Webb, who also starred in and directed, *Dragnet* was one of the longest-running and most critically acclaimed dramatic series of 1950s American television, with a phenomenal total of 263 episodes broadcast from 1952 to 1959 and a reprise (for which there was little precedent in the industry) in 1967–70 that generated 100 more programs. No doubt, Webb's police drama dominated the airwaves in the earlier decade. The initial version of the show was designed for radio, first airing in 1949 and continuing for 318 weekly episodes until 1955. Not only did the two series run concurrently for three years, they were intimately connected, with the radio scripts providing most, if not all, of the material for subsequent televisual production and broadcast. Once the move to television was made, Webb's decision to film episodes rather than to broadcast them live ensured that *Dragnet* would, because of syndication, be a continuing presence for years afterward on the small screen. In its radio and television forms, *Dragnet* left an indelible mark on American popular culture, inspiring a host of popular imitations in its own time (*The Lineup, Highway Patrol, M-Squad* and *The Untouchables* chief among them) and establishing conventions for police action programming that have been followed by the most successful series of the last three decades, including *Law and Order*, whose producer, Dick Wolf, acknowledges that "*Dragnet* is the father of us all."[1]

As critics remarked at the time, what made *Dragnet* distinctive, and popular, was its deep commitment to a form of realism that Webb borrowed, if in a substantially modified form, from the cinema, where, as a young actor, he had begun to make a name for himself in such hard-edged films as Fred Zinnemann's *The Men* (1950), Billy Wilder's *Sunset Boulevard* (1950) and Lewis Allen's *Appointment with Danger* (1951). Albert Werker's *He Walked by Night* (1949), in which Webb played a small role as a detective, exerted an especially powerful influence on his developing conception of a police procedural series, which would derive its name from the initial response to a bloody murder detailed in the film, the 'dragnet' that brings dubious characters and the usual suspects into temporary custody for questioning. The realism that *Dragnet* introduced to television violated many industry conventions, as *Variety* effusively observed when the television series was first broadcast in 1952: "There was no wasted motion, establishing the theme swiftly with racy, realistic dialog and deft locale transition. More important, there was no violence or blood-letting, and none of the artificially contrived clichés to achieve suspense."[2]

While the connection between *He Walked by Night* and Webb's radio/television series has been generally recognized, what has hitherto received little attention is the particular form of realism that Webb developed from it. It certainly could not be observed of Werker's film that it avoids 'violence or blood-letting' or eschewed 'artificially contrived clichés to achieve suspense.' It seems, instead, that Webb's desire was, as a literary critic once remarked of realist and naturalist novelists, 'to resurrect the complete illusion of real life, *using the things characteristic of real life*' (emphasis mine).[3] Despite 'borrowings' from 'the real', all fictional realisms, of course, depend on conventions, not on some special access to actuality denied to other representational traditions. The sense of lived rather than fictional experience that Webb created in *Dragnet* proves to be no exception. We may grant that here too is a confection largely dependent on techniques and consciously repeated devices that, providing the consistent stylization necessary for a long-running series to be produced on a limited budget, could easily be, and often were, effectively parodied. What is more interesting, however, is that Webb's break with the well-established traditions of radio and screen crime drama, as well as his desire to make use of the 'things characteristic of real life', were consonant with the critical protocols that elite critics of the age, enamoured of the Italian neo-realist films then such a sensational presence on the silver screen, were using to judge Hollywood movies and the various forms of television drama as well.

Successfully embodying a realistic aesthetic, *Dragnet* established its significant difference from ordinary television series, a difference ratified by its continuing popularity and appeal to the critics. A quality program, with artistic connections through its realism to the celebrated live televisual drama of the age, *Dragnet* challenges the conventional paradigm of the industry's early years of development. According to this view, the decisive break in the early history of the medium was the abandonment of single-sponsor programming in favor of network licensed shows for which advertising time was sold to various sponsors. The so-called 'Golden Age' of live drama thus made way for an era of Hollywood-produced filmed programming, which, critic William Boddy suggests, meant a repudiation of the aesthetic values promoted by prominent television critics and writers earlier in the decade. Via journalistic reviewing, technical handbooks, and general sociological criticism, writers on television in the early 1950s constructed an unusually explicit and widely shared normative aesthetics of television drama. To these critics and writers, the program changes in the mid-1950s signaled a retreat by the industry from an earlier commitment to aesthetic experimentation, program balance, and free expression.[4]

Dragnet, I would argue, complicates this simple narrative of flourishing and decline. Developed during an age of 'aesthetic commitment' and single sponsor financing, the series inaugurated a tradition of quality that did not end when the financing and production practices of the industry altered. Instead, its particular brand of realism, though reflecting the artistic values and cultural concerns of the late 1940s, has found a continuing home in the medium nearly half a century on. And that aesthetic, though partly inspired by noir films with a documentary style and feel, effects a genuine break with cinematic tradition, taking the fictional representation of criminal activity and police investigation in quite another direction.

Realism and documentary in the film noir

The immediate postwar era in Hollywood witnessed the sudden emergence of a generic hybrid: what critics of a later age have called the noir semi-documentary. Earlier entries in the hitherto somewhat slowly developing noir series had been largely based on the American *roman noir*, the high-voltage fiction of James M. Cain, Raymond Chandler, Cornell Woolrich and others, whose work was beginning to appeal to a broadly middle-class audience. These stories of seedy private investigators and murderous adulterers had been realized on screen by a visual style that owed much to the German Expressionism brought to Hollywood by a talented group of émigré directors. Films such as *Murder My Sweet* (Edward Dmytryk, 1944) and *Double Indemnity* (Billy Wilder, 1944) challenged the canons of Hollywood realism with sequences dominated by chiaroscuro lighting, strangely angled or distorted framings and an imprisoning *mise-en-scène* that served as the external correlatives of the existential dead ends to which these fatalistic narratives usually delivered their unsympathetic characters, whose world-weary cynicism found its voice in a highly stylized argot far removed from everyday speech.

Henry Hathaway's *The House on 92nd Street*, released in September 1945, a little more than a month after final victory in the Pacific, moved film noir in a substantially different direction. This wartime thriller, which is fictional only in the sense that it expands its spare story with some imagined scenes and confected dialogue, combines the visual style and formal conventions of documentary film-making with the exaggerated naturalism of the film noir, especially the genre's probing of hitherto off-limits themes and its Zolaesque preoccupation with the seedier side of contemporary American life. Produced by Louis de Rochemont, whose *March of Time* newsreels had become accustomed fare in American cinemas during the war, *The House on 92nd Street* is 'true', or at least so its authoritative narrator declares; the film re-enacts a real case of German espionage foiled during the early stages of World War II by timely and expert police work. FBI files were made available to the screenwriters. Many sequences were shot in locations around the New York City area, where the plot to steal nuclear secrets was discovered and foiled, and in Washington, D.C. at the FBI complex, where much of the investigative work on the case was done. Much of this footage is straightforwardly documentary in its apparently unstaged recording of police activities and its dispassionate description of law enforcement procedure. Non-professional actors were used in minor parts (with some of the roles being played by actual police personnel). Sequences shot silent are explained by the self-assured and omniscient narrator (Reed Hadley, in a role that he would repeat many times in subsequent films and on television).

And yet *The House on 92nd Street* is more than a re-creation of a 'true case'. The film's narrative focus is uneasily split between the Nazi agents, the fascinating perpetrators of an unfathomable and perverse evil, and their pursuers, whose unalloyed and rather flat virtue proves much less appealing, even though it naturally emerges victorious in a finale that celebrates the invincibility of American institutions. A neutral, unglamorized visual style attests to the film's accurate re-enactment of the official response to the discovered threat, but the sequences detailing the machinations of the reptilian villains strain to evoke a different atmosphere. These sequences are, as it were, overly theatrical, barely contained by Hathaway's otherwise subdued and objective approach to his material. Subsequent entrants in the noir semi-documentary manifest the same unstable melding of two opposed story worlds: the well-organized modern state, knowable as well as knowing, its irregularities surveilled and corrected by government agencies of enormous power that are always put in service of the public good; and an underworld of the maladjusted and dissatisfied, whose transgressions, moral and legal, are not only self-defeating, but otherwise easily disposed of by an unchallengeable authority.

Because of its influence through *Dragnet* on the development and subsequent history of American television in the 1950s, the most important noir semi-documentary is *He Walked by Night*, which is based on an actual case: the killing of two policemen by a fellow member of their own Pasadena, California department, who worked in the fingerprint records division. In the hands of screenwriters John C. Higgins and Crane Wilbur, this rather mundane criminal becomes a self-taught and sociopathic genius, who is not only adept at designing innovative electronic equipment, but is not above stealing what others have invented and selling it as his own. Roy Martin (Richard Basehart), unlike the pathetically inept German agents in *The House on 92nd Street*, is a cunning adversary. After he somewhat rashly kills a policeman who spots him about to burglarize an electronics shop, Martin eludes capture because he proves amazingly knowledgeable about police technique. Moreover, he is brazen enough to shoot it out with detectives who have staked out the businessman to whom he sells his inventions and stolen property. Wounded in the encounter, Martin is even possessed of the necessary sangfroid to operate successfully on himself. The police discover his hideout, yet Martin this time escapes through the Los Angeles sewer system, whose intricate twists and turnings he has made not only a private path of attack and retreat, but a hideout as well. Only a lucky chance enables the police to corner and kill him. Having once again foiled his would-be pursuers, Martin is about to escape to the dark city above when a car happens to park on the manhole cover he needs to lift up. The shotgun and stores of ammunition he had previously cached underground do him no good as he cannot triumph in a shootout against a gang of determined policemen.

He Walked by Night offers much of the same documentary stylization to be found in *The House on 92nd Street*, even though the 'case' in this film is no more than superficially based on actual events. A written title somewhat misleadingly proclaims: "This is a true story. It is known to the Police Department of one of our largest cities as the most difficult homicide case in its experience, principally because of the diabolical cleverness, intelligence and cunning of a completely unknown killer....The record is set down here factually – as it happened. Only the names are changed, to protect the innocent." These words are echoed by those of the narrator, who, as shots of Los Angeles and its police department play on the screen, provides an overview of the nation's largest urban area, whose cosmopolitanism and mixed, transient population, so he avers, provide a challenge for law enforcement. Somewhat wryly, he concludes that "the work of the police like that of woman is never done. The facts are told here as they happened." Many of the sequences in the film that detail police work are in every sense documentary, having been filmed inside the headquarters (an imposing building shot from a low angle to emphasize its embodiment of well-organized power) and furnished with an appropriate voice-over commentary. The staged sequences are carefully stylized to match the reality footage. Producers Robert Kane and Bryan Foy were so eager for authenticity that they asked the Los Angeles Police Department for a technical advisor. Sergeant Marty Wynn, who was eager to have the film avoid the distorting clichés that had dominated Hollywood treatment of crime detection, provided much valuable information about police procedure; under Wynn's tutelage, the screenwriters and performers learned the jargon of the trade, including the abbreviated language of police radio calls and the specialized vocabulary of evidence gathering and testing.

Yet it is important to note that the film, in detailing what it confesses is for the LAPD 'the most difficult homicide case in its experience', commits itself to focusing on the extraordinary rather than on the everyday aspects of police work. Influenced by film noir's preoccupation with the bizarre and the perverse, Werker and the screenwriters not surprisingly developed Roy Martin, the 'diabolical' genius, as a kind of monster who, in fact, cannot be identified and collared by ordinary police procedure. Instead, in a movement of the plot that intriguingly anticipates the spectacular finale of a more celebrated contemporary thriller, Carol Reed's *The Third Man* (1949), Martin must be hunted down and exterminated in his filthy underground lair. Werker and cinematographer John Alton, famous for his Expressionistic set-ups and visual stylization in such noir classics as *The Big Combo* (1955), *Mystery Street* (1950) and *The Hollow Triumph* (1948), put Martin in control of a shadowy alternative world, a place of darkness, anomie and reckless self-assertion that the police enter only to their peril. Detective sergeant Marty Brennan (Scott Brady) is foiled repeatedly by Martin, who seems to know police procedure better than the policeman themselves, while the criminal survives and prospers by his wits and considerable derring-do. Certainly the film's most striking scene shows the gunshot Martin removing a bullet without the benefit of either an anesthetic or medical advice. Brennan is a colourless character in comparison. Scott Brady's low-key performance in the role makes him much less dashing, energetic and resourceful than the man he seeks, played by the charismatic and attractive Richard Basehart. In fact, Brennan's failure to capture Martin after an abortive stake-out that results in the wounding of one of his partners earns him an early dismissal from the case. Only a sudden flash of inspiration persuades his chief to let him rejoin the investigation.

Martin confounds police procedure by changing what the narrator calls his 'modus operandi', transforming himself from a burglar to a robber. In his new incarnation, Martin succeeds in terrorizing the city with a series of daring liquor store robberies. The man's intimate knowledge of how the police work suggests that he is a rogue cop. His cunning duplicity revealed by police lab work (bullets fired from the cop killer's gun are shown to match one fired from the robber's), the killer is eventually, in a striking sequence, given a face by police artists who assemble the robbery victims to construct a group portrait. The patient and time-consuming check of leads provides yet another breakthrough. Martin is identified by Brennan, who wearily troops from one area police station to another looking for a match to the composite sketch. Surrounded a second time, however, the resourceful Martin manages to escape the police cordon into his sewer hideout. There he can only be stopped by his own bad luck (the blocked manhole cover) and the heroic – but group – action of the police.

The unfortunate criminal is gunned down in a shootout reminiscent of the western and the classic gangster film (such as *Public Enemy* [1931], *High Sierra* [1941] or *White Heat* [1949]). This climactic sequence provides Martin with a dramatic apotheosis, as his bullet-ridden body tumbles from a ladder into the sewage below; he suffers a literal 'fall' from power and control. Significantly, there is no closing narration to fix the meaning of this event, no celebration of the successful pursuit of a dangerous felon. The law triumphs, but that victory is not 'documented'; it is neither brought into the public realm to be adjudicated nor stylized as 'real'. The surveilling and enforcement powers of the police may prove superior (if only barely) to Martin's monstrousness, but in the clash of representational traditions the Expressionism of film noir, and not the naturalism of classic documentary, furnishes the film with its summative image.

As does the noir semi-documentary more generally, *He Walked by Night* juxtaposes a city of light (populated by citizens going about their business and watched over by the benevolent police) and a city of darkness (a criminal underworld that, metaphorized by the darkness and night that enfold it, does not easily admit the knowing, official gaze). Like the film's narrative and visual structure, the soundtrack is schizophrenic, split between the heavy, grim romantic theme that plays over Martin's lurking in the shadows and the upbeat, almost military, air that accompanies the work of the police, the grinding routine according to the 'book' that eventually identifies the criminal. The city is the focus of productive communal life (as the opening montage of shots depicting everyday life emphasizes), but its anonymous spaces shield those who, in their exceptionality, would live in defiance of officially imposed law and order. The two worlds found in the contemporary American metropolis seem utterly opposed, but they are actually strangely connected because Martin, as it turns out, is a former employee of a local police department.

And Martin is hardly, at least at the outset, a career criminal, nor is his lawbreaking to be explained sociologically. The underworld he inhabits is never figured in either economic or class terms. It seems, instead, the underside of bourgeois normality. Martin's thefts of electronic equipment are meant to further a career of invention and self-promotion for which his extraordinary mental abilities would certainly qualify him. Because he is never interrogated by the police, Martin's abandonment of a career in law enforcement remains a mystery. His former employer reveals that he left in 1942 for the military, refusing after his discharge any offer to rejoin the department. This much is clear. Eager to make a mark for himself in a postwar world driven by technological advance, inured to violence, and disposing of technical knowledge and skill gained from government service, Martin is yet another version of the returning soldier who cannot fit easily into a changed world despite his exceptional talents and energies.

The veteran mysteriously damaged by wartime service is a stock character of the film noir, an essential element of the nightmare vision of American life offered in this anti-establishmentarian Hollywood series. *He Walked by Night*, as its title suggests, is finally more interested in exploring, if not explaining, this enigmatic figure (Martin's moral nature is evoked but little through dialogue and mostly, in the Expressionist manner, by visual style and *mise-en-scène*). Despite its opening avowal of truth-telling and the narrator's commitment to setting out the facts 'as they happened', the film is much more than a straightforward chronicle of the infallible methods, the irresistible institutional power, and the quietly heroic dedication of the police to identifying and capturing criminals.

And yet it was just such a chronicle that Jack Webb intended to produce in *Dragnet* (named, significantly enough, for an investigating technique, not a monstrous villain). *He Walked by Night* provided him with a model for a police series, but Webb carefully eliminated the film's double focus on dedicated public servants and psychopathic killers, rejecting both the Expressionist stylization of film noir and the wisecracking dialogue of hard-boiled fiction.

Dragnet: A Different Kind of Realism
Webb's development of *Dragnet* is a case, to put it in Darwinian terms, of ontogeny repeating phylogeny, or, in plain language, an instance of the development of the individual replicating that of its species or type. Under the influence of the worldwide postwar fashion for realist film, noir underwent a *rapprochement* of sorts with the other

Hollywood genres that could more fully accommodate themselves to this new aesthetic. The types most affected by this new taste for and evaluation of realism were the social problem film (such as *The Men*, which treated the readjustment to civilian life of maimed veterans) or the 'small' film, which is most importantly exemplified by *Marty* [1955], a kind of anti-Hollywoodian romance. Webb's developing artistic interests show something of the same pattern of development. His two first radio dramas were firmly in the tradition of hard-boiled fiction and the classic film noir: *Pat Novak for Hire* and *Johnny Madero, Pier 13* were private eye dramas in which Webb played a tough guy detective with attitude who vented his disdain for both crooks and cops with an unending stream of elaborate wisecracks.[5]

As he often told the tale, Webb's experience on the set of *He Walked by Night* gave him a new career direction. Police officer Marty Wynn suggested that he could provide Webb with access to actual police files.[6] Webb rejected the idea at first, but soon called up Wynn, who let him ride around in his police prowler for several nights, responding to calls. Provided by Wynn and his partner with a good deal of information about police procedures and jargon, Webb decided to make authenticity the watchword of the new series that Wynn suggested could easily find its materials in the public record (names and other particulars, of course, would need to be changed in order to avoid lawsuits). In other words, the realism he was after (which could be pursued more deeply in the television version of the show) would depend not only, in the manner of Hollywood, on creating an effect of plausibility, with a view toward convincing the viewer to suspend disbelief. As we will see in detail below, Webb's realism would also be characterized by imitative precision, by the extent to which the fiction might exactly limn the contours of the real. The focus would be on the police rather than on the criminal, and the main character would be, as Webb described him, "a quiet, dedicated policeman who, as in real life, was just one little cog in a great enforcement machine. I wanted him to be an honest, decent, home-loving guy – the image of fifty thousand peace officers."[7] His Sergeant Friday was a man without much of a present or a past, whose only life was his work (a half-hearted attempt to provide him with a love interest was quickly abandoned). Certainly the access afforded by Wynn (and later by an entire grateful and supportive LAPD) to the hitherto somewhat mysterious world of police work influenced Webb substantially in his desire to tell the 'real' story of criminal investigation. But the young actor turned director and producer was likely responding as well to the critical and intellectual climate of the times. Certainly the particular fictional devices and techniques Webb selected (including a particular naturalist style of acting) owe little to what he learned from Wynn.

We have already remarked about the effect on the film noir of the wave of Italian neo-realist films that flooded the American exhibition market in the late 1940s and early 1950s. With their limited budgets and almost handmade quality, these productions, as two noted film historians have remarked, "displayed a grasp of the human condition that made Hollywood pictures seem slick and stylized." They were "filled with harsh detail" and showed "ordinary lives twisted by events and social forces beyond their control."[8]

Neorealist films were generally shot on location and with available light; they addressed topical subjects, often focusing on the experiences of those in the lower orders; plots were simple, emphasizing everyday events and avoiding both melodrama and spectacle; and unglamorous or non-professional actors were cast in featured roles, making an important connection between real and film worlds. Reviewing Roberto Rossellini's *Open City* (1946), Bosley Crowther of the *New York Times* (perhaps the era's most influential critic) praised the film for its 'overpowering realism'. *Open City*, Crowther wrote, has "the windblown look of a film shot from actualities, with the camera providentially on the scene." In part, such an aesthetic resulted from the conditions of production: "The stringent necessity for economy compelled the producers to make a film that has all the appearance and flavor of a straight documentary." More important, the neo-realist film rejects the narrative conventions of Hollywood cinema:

> The heroes in *Open City* are not conscious of being such. Nor are the artists who conceived them. They are simple people doing what they think is right. The story of the film is literal...and is said to have been based on actual facts...All these details are presented in a most frank and uncompromising way which is likely to prove somewhat shocking to sheltered American audiences...yet the total effect of the picture is a sense of real experience.[9]

Crowther also found much to praise in Vittorio De Sica's *The Bicycle Thief* (1949), a film "sharply imaged in simple and realistic terms". Here also the elaborate, Aristotelian designs of Hollywood narrative are absent, for the 'story is lean and literal, completely unburdened with "plot."' Absent too is the customary spectacle of commercial cinema: "the natural and the real are emphasized, with the film largely shot in actual settings and played by a nonprofessional cast."[10]

Among the directors who demonstrated that this kind of film could be made and marketed successfully in Hollywood was Fred Zinnemann. Jack Webb played an important supporting role in his *The Men* (1950), a chronicle of paraplegic veterans receiving treatment in a VA hospital that was independently produced by Stanley Kramer. Crowther praised Zinnemann and Kramer for creating such a 'firm, forthright, realistic study of a group of paralyzed men'. He found it noteworthy that 'much of this picture was photographed and practically all of it was derived at the Birmingham Veterans Hospital near Los Angeles.' Kramer and screenwriter Carl Foreman spent several weeks at the hospital, studying both the methods of treatment employed and the experiences of the patients, a number of whom were recruited to play minor roles in the film (the credits express gratitude to some forty-five of 'the men'). The result is that there is a 'striking and authentic documentary quality...imparted to the whole film in every detail, attitude, and word.'[11]

Like Kramer, Zinnemann and Foreman, Webb, transferring his program from radio to television, incorporated within *Dragnet* those 'things characteristic of real life', creating a fictional world that had not been seen before on the small screen, where crime shows had meant hard-boiled dramas such as *The Adventures of Ellery Queen, Martin Kane, Private Eye* and *Lights Out: Men Against Crime*, all of which were quite obviously directly descended either from the film noir, especially in its 'B' movie form, or the detective serial. Using actual cases for story material guaranteed authenticity, especially since Webb avoided exceptional crimes for the most part and eschewed violent action. In the first episode, 'The Human Bomb' (aired 16 December 1951), Friday and his partner prove able, in the nick of time, to prevent a bomber from destroying City Hall, "but this episode was a teaser whose adrenalin-pumping plot was seldom to be repeated". Subsequent episodes, though they were all titled 'The Big ____' (thus recalling notable films noirs such as *The Big Clock* [1947]), seldom depended on either fast-paced action or a deadly threat of some kind to provide audience interest even when violent criminals were being sought. Instead, the subject matter is often quite mundane, even deliberately undramatic. 'The Big Cast' (aired 14 February 1952) traces the hunt for a missing man who, once he turns up, reveals his fascination for pulp detective fiction. In 'The Big Phone Call' (aired 22 May 1952), Friday and his partner quickly corral the criminal; the bulk of the episode details their explanation to him of the police methods that led to his capture. As in the neo-realist film, the emphasis is less on a compelling narrative (even though a conventional story provides the structure for each episode) and more on the representation of the rarely viewed world of criminal investigation. Webb had no interest in creating suspenseful action; those who tuned in could depend not only on Friday and his cohorts solving every case (and emerging unscathed), but also on the judicial system never failing to convict and sentence the felons appropriately. *Dragnet*, instead, engaged viewers with what seemed to be the accurate, objective depiction of the 'truth' of police work through the re-enactment of the investigation of what is ostensibly (and usually truly is) an actual case.

Thus, the characteristic *Dragnet* scene is not physical action, such as a car chase, but conversation: sometimes the interrogation of either witnesses or suspects, sometimes a discussion among the policemen themselves about how to proceed. It is through such dialogues that the work of investigation, which is more mental than physical, can be best represented; these encounters are linked by stock footage of actual Los Angeles locations. If, as theorists of the medium have suggested, television drama, unlike the cinema, is characterized by the primacy of the soundtrack (to some degree a legacy of radio), then *Dragnet*'s refusal to emphasize action over talk is typically televisual. This seems true enough, but we should add that Webb, who had a good visual sense, animated these rather static scenes by a frequent use of extreme close-ups, filling up the small screen with the single human face in a fashion that was quite innovative and often remarked on at the time. As he said, "The close-up is the thing that pays off on the small screen...it has more impact."[12] In this way, the episode's conversational scenes were dramatized, an effect heightened by quick cross-cutting between or among speakers as well as by deftly positioned reaction shots. Dialogue, as opposed to action, scenes were, of course, also cheaper and quicker to produce, especially since Webb, always pressed for time, eschewed complicated rehearsals. Economic considerations, given the very limited budget made available, were therefore hardly negligible. But, once again, Webb was also concerned about authenticity. For the radio version of *Dragnet*, he had developed a style of delivery for his own character that he termed a 'dramatic monotone'. This might be most accurately described as a form of naturalist acting quite opposed to the 'Method' then in fashion for actors on the stage and silver screen. Relying on the then recently invented teleprompter to speed production, Webb instructed the actors to read their lines for the first time off the screen as the cameras rolled. Actors were not to 'get into the part', which Webb claimed would produce a stagy rather than realistic effect. *Dragnet* became famous for its rapid, uninflected dialogue – no more realistic, of course, than the more obvious histrionics and mumblings of the 'Method', but studiously undramatic and therefore understood by the show's audiences as more realistic.

From *He Walked by Night* and other noir semi-documentaries, Webb borrowed the device of the opening narration that attested to the show's authenticity. Every week viewers heard an authoritative voice intone: "The story you are about to see is true. Only the names have been changed to protect the innocent." In Werker's film, however, this narrator (who exists outside and apart from the story world) then also narrates the opening montage of shots of Los Angeles. Webb's innovation was to have Friday take over the narration at this point, with the lines "This is the city. Los Angeles, California." Friday thus dominates not only the world of the story, as the main character responsible for solving the case, but the manner of its telling, which is both confessional and commentative (Friday's opening remarks ironically address the anomaly of lawlessness in a city devoted to good citizenship and productive living) and officially reportorial. As narrator, Friday introduces each episode by stating the date and time, the section he is working with (burglary, traffic, etc.), and the names of his partner and commanding officer, sometimes, more informally, remarking on the weather. As each episode of the story unfolds, Friday, once again in voice-over, details the date, time and place. Such narrative commentary personalizes the narrative, but, perhaps more importantly, it offers a continuing stream of marks of authenticity, 'reality effects' that in their excessiveness (such indications of date, time, and so forth are not important to the narrative) mark it off as an ostensibly real record ('only the names have been changed...'). The concluding formula Webb devised had a similar effect. After the dramatic scenes of the investigation, the opening narrator made a second appearance, which seems even more official since his comments, which never deviate from the formula, are also printed on an insert. Like a legal notice in the paper or a court record, these provide the date and location of the trial. Each episode then closes with something like a mugshot of the malefactors, now convicts, who stand uneasily against a white background as their prison sentences (they are always found guilty) are read out. Information about their incarceration then appears below their faces, testifying to the speed and inevitability of justice being done.

Webb, it should come as no surprise, originally hoped to film *Dragnet* in LAPD headquarters. Meeting with an inevitable refusal, he set about reconstructing the building in Disney's Burbank lot, using photographs of City Hall interiors. A story, perhaps apocryphal, is that the set designers found it impossible to buy the same kind of doorknobs to be found on the office doors. Webb, however, would not be denied. He had plaster casts of the originals made so that duplicates could be manufactured. Fearful that his scriptwriters might introduce elements into the series, he hired police consultants to catch any errors. More than any police procedural series before or since, *Dragnet* was designed to incorporate those 'things characteristic of real life', bringing to the small screen the kind of imitative realism that had hitherto been found only in the cinema, and even there only in the European realist art film and its few domestic remodelings.

But the show was not content merely to show 'life' as it was. With its focus on the institutions of law enforcement rather than on individuals, *Dragnet* proffered a 'social realism' to its viewers, much as Italian neo-realist films had done with their thematic interest in the political and social difficulties of the postwar era. Such texts, theorists Julia Hallam and Margaret Marshment explain, "encourage identification not merely with characters but with the situations and events they experience", and their narratives work toward "conventional patterns of resolution and a restoration of some kind of equilibrium".[13] Perhaps the secret of its incredible popularity was that *Dragnet* not only offered the pleasures of the *tranche de vie* with an illusionism carefully constructed by the obsessive Webb; it mustered considerable rhetorical force in its support of a just society, policed by dispassionate and dedicated public servants, and served by a judiciary that accorded suitable punishment to criminals, thus preserving the rights and property of the law-abiding. Never focusing on the criminal or dramatizing the crime, *Dragnet* avoided the failed romanticism of the film noir as well as that genre's fascination with the bizarre and perverse. Through its connection to postwar realism, it discovered entertainment value as much in a potent message as in a powerfully attractive sense of authenticity, demonstrating the capacity of the new medium to provide both pleasure and instruction.

Notes

1. Quoted in Michael J. Hayde, *My Name's Friday: The Unauthorized but True Story of* Dragnet *and the Films of Jack Webb* (Nashville, TN: Cumberland House, 2001), 245.
2. Quoted in Hayde, 46.
3. W. Gerhardie, as quoted in Julia Hallam, with Margaret Marshment, *Realism and the Popular Cinema* (Manchester: Manchester University Press, 2000), 5.
4. *Fifties Television: The Industry and the Critics* (Chicago: University of Illinois Press, 199), 1–2. See further Christopher Anderson, *Hollywood TV: The Studio System in the Fifties* (Austin: University of Texas Press, 1994), 1–45.
5. For further details see Daniel Moyer and Eugene Alvarez, *Just the Facts, Ma'am: The Authorized Biography of Jack Webb* (Santa Ana, CA: Seven Locks Press, 2001), 45–53.
6. See Hayde, 18–21 and Moyer and Alvarez, 56–62.
7. Quoted in Hayde, 20.
8. Leonard J. Leff and Jerold L. Simmons, *The Dame in the Kimono: Hollywood, Censorship, and the Production Code from the 1920s to the 1960s* (New York: Doubleday, 1990), 141.
9. *New York Times* 26 February 1946.

10. *New York Times* 3 December 1949.
11. *New York Times* 21 July 1950.
12. Quoted in Hayde, 43.
13. Realism and Popular Cinema, 194.

References

(Some of the material in this chapter has been taken from an essay published in Steven Sanders and Aeon Skoble, eds, *Philosophy and TV Noir* and is re-used here with the permission of the University of Kentucky Press.)

Anderson, C., (1994): *Hollywood TV: The Studio System in the Fifties*, Austin, University of Texas Press.

Hallam, J. and Marshment, M., (2000): *Realism and the Popular Cinema* Manchester: Manchester University Press.

Hayde, M. J., (2001): *My Name's Friday: The Unauthorized but True Story of* Dragnet *and the Films of Jack Webb*, Nashville, TN: Cumberland House.

Jeff, L. J. and Simmons, J. L., (1990): *The Dame in the Kimono: Hollywood, Censorship, and the Production Code fro the 1920s to the 1960s*, New York: Doubleday.

Moyer, D. and Alvarez, E., (2001): *The Authorized Biography of Jack Webb*, Santa Ana, CA: Seven Locks Press.

New York Times, 26 February 1946.

——, 3 December 1949.

——, 21 July 1950.

THE SKILLED VIEWER

Rhona Jackson

Introduction

The audience as social construct has become the privileged premise of most television audience research. This notion has been tested on assorted audiences[1] and considerable empirical investigation,[2] and regular reviews of the field[3] have refined methodologies and methods.[4] Projects can accommodate diversity of audience, variety of text, multiplicity and diversity of visual production,[5] plus the influences of any number of factors. However, despite such advances in methodology and techniques of method, and in spite of the repeated assertion that researchers work to the idea of audience as social construct, as yet no formal model conceptualizes the television viewer specifically. In order to redress this balance, therefore, I propose here a model of the Skilled Viewer.[6] This model brings together the commonly used approach in television audience research of Uses and Gratifications, with film spectatorship theory and the model of the Informed Reader, developed in the literary field of Reader Response Theory.

Film spectatorship

Metz (1975), one of the first theorists to use Freudian psychoanalysis to explain how spectators experience film, argued that Freud's explanation of how the (male) child relates to 'the imaginary' and 'the symbolic' stages of psychic development could clarify how spectators relate to images on the cinema screen. Using Lacan's work,[7] which maintained that the unconscious is structured like language, and that use of language brings about recognition of one's own subjectivity, Metz developed the concept of the film gaze. He argued that the process of looking at a cinema screen by a spectator parallels that of the child looking into a mirror, and that watching film equates to the child's first experience of perception and recognition. Both are about becoming aware of and understanding the difference between self and image. However, where in the mirror, the child always sees its self-image, the spectator never achieves this. Rather, the spectator's gaze at the screen represents and recalls that fascination with an ideal self originally discovered in childhood and associated with the mirror-image. This memory of an ideal self discovered by looking refers the spectator back to the safety of the pre-Oedipal phase of development Freud labelled 'the imaginary', before the child is aware of himself as an individual, separate from his mother. Looking at the cinema screen becomes a desire to re-discover that self-image, which in turn relates to a repressed desire to return to and re-experience 'the imaginary'.

Metz maintained that the cinema spectator understands his own subjectivity because of his existence in 'the symbolic', the conscious state of being. Accordingly, he understands that he visits the cinema for a reason, which is to gaze at images on the screen, and he understands that images are images. Thus, Metz explained the spectator experience as: 'I know that I am perceiving something imaginary...[and] I know that it is I who am perceiving it' (1974 p. 51). He theorized the relationship of the spectator to the cinema screen as a perpetual quest for the ever-absent self-image, in order psychologically to return to the security of 'the imaginary'. However, the spectator's existence in 'the symbolic' brings about an identity conflict. The spectator's gaze actively and ceaselessly seeks the always-absent self-image, whilst, paradoxically bringing into play the desire to be lost in those images present on screen. Finally, the film gaze bestows a position of power on to the spectator, the images on screen becoming the Other.

Thus, film theorists asserted that film is predicated on the desire to look, that those who do the looking are aware that they are doing it, and that they have power over the images looked at. They related the pleasures of looking at film to Freud's initial four *scopophilic* pleasures: narcissism, voyeurism, exhibitionism and fetishism.[8]

However, useful though Metz' application of Lacan was, it was not comprehensive, as Lacan's rereading of Freudian psychoanalysis retained its male orientation, the discourse of language being patriarchal, privileging male subjectivity and the expression of phallic power. By proposing that subjectivity is socially determined by the acquisition and use of male-constructed and male-dominated language, Lacanian theory could not explain how women look. Thus, Mulvey (1975) contended that the rationale of traditional film narrative is the gratification of male heterosexual desire. As pleasures of looking are invoked from the male point of view, so mainstream films specifically address the male spectator. Narratively, the female characters are marginalized, as rewards for or on the sidelines of heroic action. Visually, they are objectified, fetishized by the use of techniques such as soft-focus lighting and close-up shots, and the general passivity of their image. Other feminist film theorists[9] proposed that Freudian psychoanalysis was over-deterministic, and that Lacanian theory focused too much on gendered subjectivity at the expense of any other social influence.

Yet, feminist critics were loath to reject psychoanalysis altogether, because it provided useful insights into psychic development and the relationship with looking generally.

They turned to object relations theory, the branch of psychoanalysis advanced by Chodorow (1978), which accommodates women's and men's experience equally. Chodorow agreed that subjectivity is socially constructed, but not that an individual's psyche is solely determined by their inevitable position within a patriarchal linguistic structure. Social relationships must be considered to be key influences in psychic development, the pre-Oedipus phase being as important a learning experience as is the Oedipus phase. But, where Freud argued that the point when the male child realizes his separateness is crucial for his individual development, Chodorow maintained that for little girls their 'connectedness' to others is the significant issue, the negotiation of the Oedipus phase being more complicated for girls.

Chodorow's theories equipped critics with the means to escape the linear perspective of traditional Freudian psychoanalysis, to point up the polysemic nature of the visual text, and to show that women were positioned differently from men in relation to the text. Hers became the privileged approach for theorists concentrating on texts which appeared to address female viewers, the 'women's genres'.[10] Object relations theory enabled the needs of female protagonists to be considered and permitted the investigation of that 'strong tradition of resistance' (Byars 1988 p. 217) in both film and television, which traditional psychoanalysis could not acknowledge because it was trapped by its determinist norm of the male/masculine point of view.

Feminist critics also applied Chodorow to television texts[11] with results which permitted female viewers equivalent experiences of identification and desire, originally associated with the male film spectator.

So, theoretical developments within film spectatorship theory are relevant here, in terms of the acknowledgement of psychic development, desire and gendered spectatorship and the application to televisual texts. But, the model's lack of empirical testing[12] means it falls short of a comprehensive explanation of the television viewer. In contrast, the Uses and Gratifications approach to the television audience is based on empirical research.

Uses and Gratifications
This model's insistence on the active, socially constituted, self-aware audience and systematic research techniques has proved repeatedly effective. Katz, Blumler and Gurevitch (1974) argued[13] for a statement of function whose fundamental principle is that mass media use gratifies audience needs, Uses and Gratifications contends that the active viewer makes a conscious and purposeful selection of specific programmes to satisfy particular identifiable needs. Then, McQuail (1983) added that all audience response to every type of television programme could be systematically summarized under one of four categories: Personal Identity; Integration and Social Interaction; Entertainment; and Information; each of which could be subdivided to allow responses to be described as precisely as possible.

Moreover, being a grounded theory, as weaknesses in the Uses and Gratifications model are identified, so researchers review and amend the model.[14] For example, Morley's questioning of how effectively the notion of the 'preferred reading'[15] of the text could be applied to 'fictional' as well as 'factual' texts, resulted in him arguing that such notion was not sufficiently comprehensive to account for variations in responses to texts other than the factual.[16] The analytical focus should instead be shifted on to the diverse forms of 'cultural competence' which audiences bring to bear on distinct forms of television.[17] McQuail developed this further, advising that researchers should vary their approach depending on why the audience used the mass media, 'observ[ing] a closer distinction between 'cognitive' and 'cultural' types of content and media use' (1987 p. 237) and the corresponding different types of gratifications. Katz, Blumler and Gurevitch's original explanation of the Uses and Gratifications model as needs-use-gratification was ultimately understood to be too restrictive, researchers realizing that explaining effects by making a distinction between mass media use and need gratification was especially difficult. Accordingly, McQuail revised the statement of function to read as follows:

> (1) Personal social circumstances and psychological dispositions together influence both (2) general habits of media use and also (3) beliefs and expectations about the benefits offered by the media, which shape (4) specific acts of media choice and consumption, followed by (5) assessment of the value of the experience (with consequence for further media use) and, possibly (6) application of benefits acquired in other areas of experience. (Ibid. p. 235)

Thus, similar to the way film spectatorship theory developed to incorporate more than the male spectator, so Uses and Gratifications developed from a linear, functional model of needs-use-gratification, to one which can incorporate notions of audience expectation, too.[18]

Despite such developments, however, Uses and Gratifications remains theoretically inadequate on the explanatory level. For instance, McQuail's categories of response tend to be descriptive rather than explanatory. Identification, for example, is a description, not an explanation of one type of gratification. And the comparison with the lived experience of the audience is illustration only of *how* gratification is sought and obtained. *Why* viewers may wish to look like television performers, or seek reassurance from seeing their own roles mirrored on television, are questions that Uses and Gratifications cannot adequately explain.

However, as audience response to film and television were being explored, so debates about the literary audience were taking place, which led to the development of theoretical models of readership, which could also be empirically tested.

Reader Response Theory
Such models were developed by, for example, Iser (1976)[19] and Fish (1976), whose model was used to explain reader engagement with *popular* as well as *quality*

literature.[20] Fish conceptualized the model of the Informed Reader to account for difference(s) in reading competence:

> The informed reader is someone who (1) is a competent speaker of the language out of which the text is built up; (2) is in full possession of 'the semantic knowledge that a mature...listener brings to his task of comprehension', including the knowledge (that is, the experience, both as a producer and comprehender) of lexical sets, collocation probabilities, idioms, professional and other dialects, and so on; and (3) has literary competence. That is, he is sufficiently experienced as a reader to have internalised the properties of literary discourses, including everything from the most local of devices (figures of speech, and so on) to whole genres...this informed reader [is] neither an abstraction nor an actual living reader, but a hybrid – a real reader (me) who does everything within his power to make himself informed. (1980 pp. 48–9)

The literary competence of the Informed Reader is dependent on a linguistic competence which includes the ability to use language diversely for a variety of purposes, plus, as the film spectator understands what they do when they look, so the Informed Reader understands their differentiated use of language. To account for variations in reader-competence and how one reader may read different texts in a variety of ways, and, correspondingly, why a number of readers may read a single text in the same way, Fish introduced the notion of *interpretive communities*. He defined interpretive communities as such because they share a repertoire of *interpretive strategies*, explaining that

> both the stability of interpretation among readers and the variety of interpretation in the career of a single reader would seem to argue for the existence of something independent of and prior to interpretive acts, something which produces them. I will answer this challenge by asserting that both the stability and the variety are functions of interpretive strategies rather than of text. (Ibid. p. 168)

Interpretive strategies are the result of a reader's socio-cultural experience, '[d]ifferent readers agree[ing] on the same interpretive strategies because they belong to interpretive communities' (Ibid. p. 171). A single reader can operate separate and distinct interpretive strategies depending on with which of several memberships of interpretive communities they choose to identify. For example, Fish regarded the literary critic as no higher in status than those readers whom traditional literary critics describe as naïve (note the inclusion in his quotation: 'a real reader (me)....' All readers are *Informed Readers*, all readings granted equal validity, the only difference being convention of interpretive strategy. As a literary critic, he inferred meaning from a text because of those conventions of literary criticism which are interpretive strategies learnt from membership of the interpretive community of literary critics. Other readers are guided by their own conventions, by shared interpretive strategies learnt from their respective interpretive communities. Fish's methodology was to examine the reading experience, defined as his own and others' responses to a text, in a step-by-step procedure. For instance, he illustrated how, when criticizing poetry, he habitually noticed line-endings; they held meaning for him, so he attributed meaning to them. Other readers would observe other factors from which they make meaning and to which they attach value.

So, the Informed Reader is a self-aware, self-monitoring subject, who may belong to more than one interpretive community. Hence, a single reader may employ more than one interpretive strategy not only to read different texts, but to read one text at different times, how they read depending upon the experience they associate with previous readings and the membership of whichever interpretive community upon which they call at the time of reading. The notion of interpretive strategies explains how several readers may read a single text in the same way, plus how a single reader may read one text on separate occasions in quite contradictory ways, justified within the terms of the interpretive community they use as a frame of reference.

In contrast, therefore, to film theory's relegation of the spectator to theoretical abstract, Reader Response Theory emphasizes the reader as site of study, challenges the traditional critical attention to the author and the text and argues against the conventional tendencies of literary criticism to treat readers as naïve and proclaim the literary critic's interpretation to be skilled, objective and of higher value.

Thus, three aspects of Fish's Informed Reader are pertinent here: the notion of differentiated reader-competence, the significance of the act of reading and the systematic approach to readers. Inherent within the notion of the self-observant Informed Reader is that the reader approaches the literary text as in a quest for knowledge. By observing and monitoring their own responses, readers learn, become better informed and more competent to deal with the current text and, subsequently, with successive texts. The Informed Reader is conceptualized as positive, active, self-aware, possessing competence which improves via exposure to texts. Thus, the essence of the Informed Reader, the notion of interpretive communities sharing interpretive strategies, could be usefully adapted to the experiences of the television viewer. As Fish's assumption that the Informed Reader actively and knowingly engages with the text reinforces the significance of the subjective reading experience in the construction of meaning. This centrality of the reader and structured approach to the reader, matches the key concerns of the Uses and Gratifications approach which regards the viewing experiences and the viewers' reports of those experiences as similarly valuable.

Radway's application of Fish (1984) also demonstrated the effectiveness of the Informed Reader and proved to be a critical contribution to the development of the Skilled Viewer.

The Informed Reader Applied
Radway applied and developed Fish's model. She reviewed the romantic novel publishing industry, her readers' descriptions of romances, and examined the traditional language and narrative strategies of romantic fiction. Crucially, she explored the act of

reading the romance itself and the explanations the women readers gave of it. Her investigation proceeded in four stages: questionnaire; discussion; analysis; interpretation. The questionnaire established the sociocultural and familial influences on readers, taking account of factors they deemed significant, but which she had not initially considered. She followed this with in-depth discussions on the romance. Then, her structural analysis of a number of romances was directed by the topics foregrounded by the readers. Thus, she identified what romance readers seek from the romance novel, constructing the 'ideal romance' and the 'failed romance' from their point of view. Like the feminist film theorists, she used Chodorow to interpret her reader response. Throughout, Radway used an ethnographic account in order to report her findings systematically and objectively, whilst simultaneously ensuring that it coincided with and would be recognized by her readers.

Radway's research subjects were drawn from an interpretive community of romance readers living in a single region of the USA to illustrate how social contextualization bears on cultural experience. She insisted that the readers' existence as social beings be the descriptive cornerstone of the readership subject position. Being interpreters of texts was the pre-eminent constituent of that subject position because it was via their responses to the romances that their attitudes and beliefs were revealed.

Emphasizing the primacy of reader perception prevented Radway from falling into the trap identified by Fish as a fault of traditional literary critics, and encountered also by television audience researchers: that of valuing her own reading of the text above that of the reader. Her ethnographic account bestowed critical distance on the necessarily intimate methods of data collection. She structured her research approach within an anthropological framework traditionally used to research alien cultures,[21] focusing on her readers' subjective experience within the context of their daily lives, her own reading experience being secondary. Thus, she avoided any decline into personal obsession and theoretical chaos, previously cited as a potential problem with Fish's model.[22] Plus, her methods forbade her to impose any 'preferred reading' on to her audience. By systematically referring from readers to text and back to readers, she constructed the common interpretation that was the audience reading. Her analysis, directed by her readers, was as little contaminated as possible by her own opinions.

Readership, Spectatorship, Uses and Gratifications: Conceptualizing the Skilled Viewer
Like Radway's examination of the act of reading, the conventions of television audience research have evolved so that what constitutes the viewing process has become the focus of investigation. Yet, where Radway investigated the readership of one literary genre, increasingly in television audience research the focus has shifted to investigate the nature of viewing in general. Plus, viewers, too, can be understood to belong to interpretive communities, it being incumbent on researchers to relate the interpretations of text as far as possible to viewers' experiences as members of these socially constituted groups who hold shared *interpretive repertoires*. Consequently, I should argue that the focus should be shifted from interpretive communities, which prioritizes the

membership of such, effectively narrowing the research focus, to those shared interpretive repertoires. The audience is still located socially, but the focus centres on interpretation. So, the audience is conceptualized to be 'formal groups or communities, but contextually defined agents who employ such repertoires to make preliminary sense' (Jankowski and Wester 1991, p. 62).

This would take account of Morley and Silverstone's (1991) insistence on the significance of the viewing context and researcher reflexivity. Plus, it has long been understood how material conditions of film exhibition and television broadcasting affect audience response,[23] the principal differences concerning the amount of control the immediate environment exerts on the viewing experience. Comparing film spectatorship with television viewing, for example, the gaze of the cinema spectator is drawn to the film because of the size of and remoteness of the screen, the darkness of the auditorium and so on. In contrast, the domestic familiarity of television obliges it to compete for attention with many other distractions, Ellis (1982) arguing that it needs more than visual appeal, relying greatly on sound to 'hook' the viewer. Similarly, I assume here that sound is fundamental to the understanding of all visual images, as in both film and television, sound works in conjunction with the image to suggest certain interpretations. So, comedy dialogue works with the image to promote a particular type of (humour-related) response, talk shows focus on talk and, thus, on listening. Such programmes provide material for viewers to take away with them and feed the 'culture' which surrounds television production and consumption. For instance, several studies into film[24] and television[25] have found that gossip and notions of fandom are key constituents of audience appreciation.

Thus, film spectatorship, Uses and Gratifications and Reader Response Theory have the same end in view: to explore and understand the text/audience relationship. All set out from contradictory standpoints so the means to that end differ. Film theory's spectator is a purely theoretical individual. Reader Response Theory considers the active individual reader-as-practitioner. Uses and Gratifications addresses the active viewer-as-social-subject and user of the text. What is considered as evidence varies also. Film theory hypothesizes in abstraction from reality how a spectator's understanding is processed and why certain interpretations prevail. Reader Response Theory examines the actual practice of interpretation, the act of reading. Uses and Gratifications investigates how people use the medium they choose, the latter two drawing conclusions from users' own accounts of their experiences.

This model, adopted and adapted from three approaches, can be explained in the way Fish explained the Informed Reader as follows:

> The Skilled viewer is someone who (1) is a competent speaker of the language out of which the text is built up; (2) is in full possession of the semantic knowledge that a mature listener brings to his/her task of comprehension, including the knowledge (that is, the experience, both as a producer and comprehender) of lexical sets,

collocation probabilities, idioms, professional and other dialects, and so on; and (3) is a competent television viewer. That is, he/she is sufficiently experienced as a viewer to have internalised the properties of television discourses, including everything from the most local of devices (theme tune, announcements, outside broadcasts) to whole genres. (4) He/she is also aware of performance criteria (that fictional characters are depicted by actors acting, for instance). (5) The Skilled viewer views television from a social and familial position structured by social class and gender, a position which influences their preference for, expectations of, and access to television programmes. This Skilled viewer is neither an abstraction nor an actual living viewer, but a hybrid – a socially constituted, active viewer (any one of us) who views television for a variety of reasons, those associated with entertainment, information, personal identity, and integration and social interaction likely to be the most significant.

The Skilled Viewer

	Film Theory	Reader Response Theory	Uses and Gratifications Theory
Basic Assumption	Dominant sociocultural values govern those conventions which direct mainstream film production;	The reader is the prime agent in the construction of meaning;	The audience uses the text to gratify a need;
Theoretical framework	Abstract model of the spectator experience;	A model of the actual reading experience;	A model of the actual viewing experience;
Objective	To shed light on the text/ audience relationship;	To shed light on the text/ audience relationship;	To shed light on the text/ audience relationship;
Methodology: a: Subject: Examining whom?	Individual theoretical spectator;	Individual 'real' reader;	'Real' socially constituted reader/viewer;
b: Evidence: Examining what?	Analyst's opinion of spectator experience;	Reader's account of reading experience;	Audience account of viewing experience;
c: Explanatory devices: How is evidence interpreted?	Psychoanalytic tools refined and reworked by feminist theorists.	Subjective analysis refined and reworked by practical application.	Tools not yet fully developed.

Figure 1. Clarifies how the three approaches come together[26] to explain the television viewer.

Notes

1. See, for instance, McQuail, Blumler and Brown (1972); Morley (1980; 1981); Hobson (1982).
2. See, for example, Buckingham (1987, 1995); Seiter et al. (1991); Gauntlett and Hill (1998).
3. See Morley (1992, 1996); Ang (1996), Dickinson et al. (1998); Ross and Nightingale (2004).
4. Particularly interesting here are the works of McQuail (1969, 1972, 1983, 2000).
5. Just as film spectatorship initially influenced television audience research, so, for instance, the latter is the basis for much video and Internet audience research. Plus, empirical study of the film spectator (see Barker and Brooks 1998) is being introduced into the discipline of film studies.
6. This model was originally developed for my Ph.D. in 1993.
7. See Mitchell and Rose (1983).
8. Narcissism, being obsessed with one's own self-image, becomes for the spectator obsession with looking at an image with which they want to identify. Voyeurism, the child's overwhelming curiosity to see their parents' genitals/their parents having sex, translates into the desire to gaze at others, when the gazer is unseen and the gazed-at are, or behave as though they are unaware of being watched. Exhibitionism, taking pleasure in being looked at, relates to identification with an image specifically as an image-to-be-looked-at. Fetishism, when a person is objectified by being sexually represented by a body part in order to defuse any 'threat' the objectifier may experience is, for the spectator, when images of women on screen simultaneously represent the Other and become phallic substitutes.
9. See Cowie (1978); Kuhn (1982, 1984); Modleski (1982); Byars (1988).
10. See Byars (1988).
11. See Modleski (1983); Gamman and Marshment (eds) (1988).
12. See Meeres (2004).
13. Basic assumptions are: [a] The audience is conceptualized as active. Consequently, [b] there is no assumption of any direct effect on audience beliefs, attitudes or behaviour; [c] the mass media are obliged to compete with other sources of need gratification; [d] the audience is sufficiently self-aware adequately to report back on why they use the mass media as they do; [e] the audience perspective is accorded priority, the analyst suspending judgement until thorough investigation of audience response has been completed. (Summary of Katz, Blumler and Gurevitch 1974: 21.)
14. See, for instance, Blumler and Katz (1974); McQuail (1987); Ang (1985).
15. The 'preferred reading' expresses the dominant ideological viewpoint of the society in which it is produced. This is understood by all viewers from that society who may agree with, reject, or challenge it depending on the socio-cultural influences to which they are exposed in/by their position in society.
16. Morley (1981) concluded this after reviewing his own research into the UK current affairs television programme, *Nationwide*.
17. Morley (1992) explains how the use of the concept of the 'preferred reading' has developed in audience research.
18. See, for instance, Rayburn and Palmgreen's studies (1985).
19. Iser's model of the Implied Reader assumed that there are messages encoded in a text whose meanings await activation by a decoding reader, the text offering several different meanings for the reader to take up. The Implied Reader results from a tension between 'the textual

structure' and 'the structured act of reading' (1976 p. 34), the reader being allowed a degree of power in the construction of meaning. There will always be a tension between the Implied Reader and the real reader, the human subject of which the Implied Reader is but one dimension.
20. See Radway (1984).
21. For an explanation of Radway's anthropological framework, see Berry and Dasen (1974).
22. This was a particular criticism levelled at Fish by Iser.
23. See Elsaesser (1981); Ellis (1982).
24. See Barker and Brooks (1998) re the spectators for the film *Judge Dredd*.
25. See Jenkins (1992); Livingstone and Lunt (1994).
26. I acknowledge that because of their respective aims and objectives that the theories are unlikely to work together without tension. However, I suggest that they can integrate sufficiently effectively, bringing together the abstract theory of the film spec for these, implying they meant he/she? I don't think this is necessary, but I could not remove the 'paintbrush' effect. Thanks.

References

Ang, I., (1985): *Watching Dallas: Soap Opera and the Melodramatic Imagination*, London, Methuen.

Ang, I., (1996): *Living Room wars: Rethinking Audiences for a Postmodern World*, London, Routledge.

Barker, M. and Brooks, K., (1998): *The Knowing Audience: Judge Dredd: Its Friends, Fans and Foes*, Luton, University of Luton Press.

Berry, J. W. and Dasen, P. R. (eds), (1974): *Culture and Cognition: Readings in Cross-cultural Psychology*, London, Methuen.

Betterton, R. (ed.), (1987): *Looking On: Images of Femininity in the Visual Media*, London, Harper Collins.

Blumler, J. G, and Katz, E. (eds), (1974): *The Uses of Mass Communications: Current Perspectives in Gratifications Research*, London, Sage.

Buckingham, D., (1987): *Public Secrets: EastEnders and its Audience*, London, British Film Institute.

——, (1995): *Moving Images: Understanding Children's Emotional Responses to Television*, Manchester, Manchester University Press.

Byars, J., (1988): 'Gazes/Voices/Power: Expanding Psychoanalysis for Feminist Film and Television Theory'. In D. E. Pribram (ed.): *Female Spectators: Looking at Film and Television*, London and New York, Verso.

Chodorow, N., (1978): *The Reproduction of Mothering: Psychoanalysis and the Sociology of Gender*, Berkeley, University of California Press.

Cowie, E., (1978): 'Woman as Sign', in *m/f* (1), pp. 49–63.

de Lauretis, T., (1987): *Alice Doesn't: Feminism, Semiotics and Cinema*, Basingstoke, Macmillan.

Dickinson, R., Harindranath, R. and Linné, O. (eds), (1998): *Approaches to Audiences: A Reader*, London, Arnold.

Ellis, J., (1982): *Visual Fictions*, London, Routledge.

Elsaesser, Thomas, (1982): 'Visual Pleasure and Audience Oriented Aesthetics' (originally delivered as a seminar paper for the Educational Advisory Service of the British Film

Institute, 1969), in T. Bennett, S. Boyd-Bowman, C. Mercer and J. Woollacott (eds): *Popular Television and Film*, London, British Film Institute.

Fish, S., (1980): *Is there a text in this class? The authorities of Interpretive Communities*, (originally published 1976), Cambridge, Harvard University Press.

Freud, S., (1977): *The Interpretation of Dreams* (originally published 1900), London, Penguin.

——, (1974): *Introductory Lectures on Psychoanalysis* (originally published 1917), London, Penguin.

Gamman, L. and Marshment, M. (eds), (1988): *The Female gaze: Women as Viewers of Popular Culture*, London, The Women's Press.

Gauntlett, D. and Hill, A., (1998): *TV Living: Television, Culture and Everyday Life*, London, Routledge.

Hobson, D., (1982): Crossroads: *The Drama of a Soap Opera*, London, Methuen.

Jackson, R., (1993): *Situation Comedy and the Female Audience: A Case Study of* The Mistress, Sheffield Hallam University, unpubd.

Iser, W., (1976): *The Act of Reading: a Theory of Aesthetic Response*, Baltimore, Johns Hopkins University Press.

Jankowski, N. W. and Wester, F., (1991): 'The qualitative tradition in social science inquiry: contributions to mass communication research'. In K. B. Jensen, and N. W. Jankowski (eds): *A Handbook of Qualitative Methodologies for Mass Communication Research*, London, Routledge.

Jenkins, H., (1992): *Textual Poachers: Television Fans and Participatory Cultures*, London, Routledge.

Kaplan, E. A., (1983): *Regarding Television*, Berkeley, American Film Institute.

Katz, E., Blumler, J. G. and Gurevitch, M., (1974): 'Utilization of Mass Communication by the Individual'. In Blumler and Katz (eds) op. cit.

Kuhn, A., (1982): *Women's Pictures: Feminism and Cinema*, London, RKP.

——, (1984): 'Women's Genres'. In *Screen* (25) 18, pp. 18–25.

Livingstone, S. and Lunt, P., (1994): *Talk on Television: Audience Participation and Public Debate*, London, Routledge.

McQuail, D., (1969): 'The Audience for One Act Plays'. In J. Tunstall (ed.): *Media Sociology*, London: Constable, 1969.

——, (1972): *Sociology of Mass Communications*, Harmondsworth, Penguin Books Ltd.

——, (1983): *Mass communication Theory: An Introduction*, London, Sage.

——, (2000): *Mass Communication Theory* (4th edn), London, Sage.

Meeres, P., (2001): 'Is There an Audience in the House?' In *Journal of Popular Culture*, (Fall).

Metz, C., (1975): 'The Imaginary Signifier'. In *Screen*, (16) 2, pp. 14–76.

Mitchell, J. and Rose, J., (1983): *Feminine Sexuality: Jacques Lacan et l'École Freudiènne*, London, Macmillan.

Modleski, T., (1982): *Loving with a Vengeance: Mass Produced Fantasies for Women*, London, Methuen.

——, (1983): 'The Rhythms of Reception: Daytime Television and Women's Work'. In Kaplan (ed.), op. cit.

Morley, D., (1980): *The Nationwide Audience*, London, British Film Institute.

——, (1981): 'Nationwide: A Critical Postscript'. In *Screen Education* (Summer) 30, pp. 6–18.

——, (1992): *Television, Audiences and Cultural Studies*, London, Routledge.

——, (1996): 'Populism, revisionism and the 'new' audience research. In Curran, J., Morley, D. and Walkerdine, V. (eds): *Cultural studies and communication.* London, Arnold, pp. 279–83.

Morley, D. and Silverstone, R., (1991): 'Communication and context: ethnographic perspectives on the media audience'. In K. B. Jensen, and N. W. Jankowski (eds): *A Handbook of Qualitative Methodologies for Mass Communication Research*, London, Routledge.

Palmgreen, P. and Rayburn, J. D., (1985): 'An Expectancy-Value Approach to Media Gratifications'. In *Mass Communications Research*, K. E. Rosengren et al. (eds), London, Sage.

Radway, J. A., (1984): *Reading the Romance: Women, Patriarchy, and Popular Literature*, Chapel Hill, University of North Carolina Press.

Rayburn, J. D. and Palmgreen, P., (1985): 'Merging Uses and Gratifications and Expectancy-Value Theory'. In *Mass Communications Research*, K. E. Rosengren et al. (eds), London, Sage.

Ross, K. and Nightingale, V., (2004): *Media and Audiences: New Perspectives*, Maidenhead, Open University Press.

Seiter, E., Borchers, H., Kreutzner, G. and Worth, E. (eds), (1991): *Remote Control: Television Audiences and Cultural Power*, London, Routledge.

THE CULTURE OF POST-NARCISSISM: POST-TEENAGE, PRE-MIDLIFE SINGLES CULTURE IN SEINFELD, ALLY MCBEAL AND FRIENDS

Michael Skovmand

In an article a few years ago, David P. Pierson makes a persuasive case for considering American television comedy, and sitcoms in particular, as 'Modern Comedies of Manners'. These comedies afford a particular point of entry into contemporary mediatized negotiations of 'civility', i.e. they are concerned with the way in which individual desires and values interface with the conventions and standards of families, peer groups and society at large (Pierson 2000). The apparent triviality of subject matter and the hermetic appearance of the groups depicted may deceive the unsuspecting media researcher into believing that these comedies are indeed 'shows about nothing'. The following is an attempt to take Pierson's general point further, in an assessment of a particular range of contemporary American television comedies as sites of ongoing negotiations of behavioural anxieties within post-teenage, pre-midlife singles culture – a culture which in many aspects seems to articulate central concerns of society as a whole. This range of TV comedies can also be seen, in a variety of modes, to point to new ways in which contemporary television comedy articulates audience relations and relations to contemporary culture as a whole.

American television series in the past twenty-five years have embodied the time-honoured American continental dichotomy between the West Coast and the East Coast. The West Coast – LA – signifies the Barbie dolls of *Baywatch* and the overgrown high school kids of *Beverly Hills 90210*. On the East Coast – more specifically New York or Boston, a sophisticated tradition of television comedy has developed since the early 1980s far removed from the beach boys and girls of California. It is grown-up – or almost grown-up television comedy, it is urban, and its roots are not the feel-good world of the Beach Boys, but the narcissistic conversational culture of Woody Allen.

The beginning – to the extent that one can talk about beginnings of genres that reach back into radio and beyond – was *Cheers*, the mother of recent sitcoms, which ruled the American networks between 1982 and 1993, becoming the greatest success series in American television history. The cosy Boston bar was home away from home to a handful of employees and regulars, plus whoever walked through the door, presided over by the ever-present Sam (Ted Danson), ex-baseball player with an ever vigilant eye on the main chance. *Cheers* gave us fast-paced adult talk, breaking new ground in conversational permissiveness and precision. But even this loosely constructed sitcom machine gradually depleted its narrative repertoire, and the defunct concept was milked by a number of spin-offs, notably *Frazier*. The real inheritor, however, was Jerry Seinfeld, the stand-up comedian of *Saturday Night Live* fame, who, along with Larry David created *Seinfeld* (NBC, 1989–98) in 1989, a sitcom that was to rival *Cheers* both in terms of humorous acuity and cult status. The series is based on two extraordinary gimmicks: Seinfeld plays himself, and the series pretends to be about nothing. Each episode (except for the last two seasons) is framed by stand-up monologue by Jerry himself, but the major attraction is the ensemble situation comedy of the four single friends, Jerry, George (Jason Alexander), Kramer (Michael Richards) and Elaine (Julia Louis -Dreyfus), either in their favourite coffee-shop booth or in Jerry's small New York apartment, complete with the classic sitcom sofa facing the live audience, and a repertoire of running gags such as next-door neighbour Kramer's sliding sideways entrances.

Whereas *Seinfeld* is deliberately unglamorous, *Friends* (NBC, 1994–2003) is far more yuppie-oriented – or, perhaps, post-yuppie-oriented. It is the story of six personable New York singles – three of each sex – neighbours in the same apartment building, and again the majority of the scenes are played out either in one of the apartments or on the sitcom sofa of the nearby coffee shop, Central Perk. Metaphorically speaking, *Friends* can be seen as a sequel to *Family Ties*, the famous 1980s sitcom, in which the nuclear family still existed, albeit in slightly parodic post -1968-ish version. *Friends* is where Alex (Michael J. Fox) – again metaphorically speaking – can be seen to have moved to, after he moved away from his hippie parents in disgust. He has subsequently recognized the limitations of the 80s Reaganite yuppie culture and has sought refuge in the quasi-commune of apartment-clustered single friends. In fact, Monica (Courtney Cox) of *Friends* is Alex's sometime girlfriend from *Family Ties*.

Whereas *Seinfeld* determinedly undermines any tendency towards the emotional, *Friends* is a story about friendship among singles as a haven in an adult world full of demands, sexual, careerwise and otherwise – a haven in which the six singles are encapsulated in a bubble of security, from which would-be boyfriends and girlfriends are constantly assessed by the collective and found wanting. This Peter Pan world of *Friends* is strong on understated dialogue and ironic repartee, but veers back and forth between ironic detachment and sentimentality – a reflection of the dilemma of the series as a whole which is: how seriously to take the lifestyle problems of these post-adolescent characters.

Ally McBeal (FOX, 1997–2002) has taken this dilemma further. The makeshift sitcom format has been scrapped in favour of what is simply termed 'comedy', which is to say no live audience, more production value, i.e. a more expensive and more edited production. With Calista Flockhart as the near-anorexic protagonist, Ally (her weight problems and her potentially negative influence as a role model are seriously debated in American media), David Kelley, with a track record of unorthodoxy from series such as *Picket Fences* and *Chicago Hope*, has produced a post-feminist psychodrama, which takes the neuroses of post-adolescent singlehood to new heights of intensity. Set in a male-owned, but female-dominated firm of lawyers in Boston with unisex toilets – at times there is more action in the toilets than in the offices – the courtroom drama, more often than not, is upstaged by the sexual and emotional conflicts among the employees. Whereas *Seinfeld* is predominantly, if low-key, Jewish, and Friends generally white urban, *Ally McBeal* reverts to the standard American serial ethnic mix, including both a Chinese and a black lawyer – both women – but apart from that the series is resolutely politically incorrect. To give an example: Ling, the Chinese woman lawyer at one point snarls angrily at a man in a wheelchair who gets in her way, adding, as an aside, "...as if you are not already getting all the good parking spots..."

In *Ally McBeal*, the invasion of the workplace by the personal sphere has been taken to extremes, frequently drowning out any sense that any real work is going on at all. On top of that, the series has inaugurated a surrealistic visual dimension, in which particularly Ally's fantasies of sex, inferiority and motherhood are literalized in the form of digitized visual manipulations – reducing Ally to half size, extending her tongue by a foot, or introducing hallucinations of the babies she has never had. Courtroom drama, when it does occur, has moved a long way from the concerned realism of such series as *LA. Law* – at one point there is a case brought against God – veering between crazy screwball comedy and unbridled emotionality, often parodying the excesses of litigious American legal culture. One further entertaining dimension about *Ally McBeal* is its massive use of oldies pop music, either performed by singer-pianist Vonda Shephard or through cameo appearances of singers such as the late Barry White, whose performance of 'My First, My Last, My Everything' on the show meant a relaunching of the career of the old crooner. Indeed, the use of oldies pop music is consistently used to signify the nostalgic dimension of the emotional archive of the entire cast – nostalgia and neurosis being the overriding mindsets of the *Ally McBeal* environment. In this post-Freudian self-reflexive environment, the services of psychoanalysts are of little help. This post-yuppie generation knows on'ly too well all the explanatory models of repression, displacement, early childhood trauma etc.

The characters of all three series are – with variations – caught in what Christopher Lasch as early as 1979, in the well-established vein of American cultural pessimism, identified as the Culture of Narcissism. They are beyond the civil rights movements, Vietnam,

Watergate and the yuppie optimism of the Reagan era, no longer with any confidence in the larger emancipatory creeds their parents and grandparents clung to. In their place there is a restless individualism, a post-ironic self-consciousness and a peer group of post-adolescent friends. Larger concepts such as 'society', 'politics' or 'justice' are not totally jettisoned, but are seen as problematic, compromised as they are by the rhetoric of the parent generation. Instead, there is a deliberate minimalism, where the emotional minutiae of the personal world are magnified into ironically gigantic proportions. All the characters are locked into what – since Gregory Bateson – has been referred to as a *double bind*: a powerful yearning towards and an equally strong fear against 'commitment' – to permanent relationships, to parenthood, to a sense of purpose beyond themselves. And the biological clock – a recurrent fearful image in the series – keeps ticking away. As Jerry Seinfeld, as 'Jerry', phrases it: "What's wrong with us? Why aren't we married? Why don't we have wives and children? Why are we not men like our fathers?"

Seinfeld: No hugging, no learning
It is my contention in this essay that *Seinfeld* in particular has taken this minimalism to exceptionally interesting lengths. The following is an attempt to characterize this situation comedy – officially defunct, but with a vigorous afterlife in worldwide syndication – as one of the defining televisual events of the 1990s.

A short history of *Seinfeld*
Seinfeld is a show which is firmly rooted in stand-up comedy. It is the exclusive creation of two people with extensive stand-up experience – Jerry Seinfeld and Larry David, and their background in shows such as the illustrious *Saturday Night Live* is felt in all aspects of the show, from the unorthodoxy of ideas to the irreverence of treatment of themes.

The pilot – *The Seinfeld Chronicles* – aired in 1989 – already contains the major ingredients of the show as we know it: Jerry Seinfeld's introductory and concluding stand-up routines, the two major locations: the coffee shop and Jerry's apartment and the absurd focus on conversational minutiae. Kramer (named Kessler in this first episode) is already in character, preoccupied with the contents of Jerry's fridge, and the story with its main focus on the etiquette of dating is recognizably Seinfeldian.

The only element missing is the female character – Elaine – who is introduced in the next episode, (the show, according to Jerry Seinfeld, 'lacked estrogen' (Gattuso 1998: 136)), making up the foursome that was to be the defining main cast for the next nine years.

The show was no immediate success – in fact, the tribulations of the show can be paralleled to those of another quirky, groundbreaking show of the early 1980s, *Hill Street Blues*, as chronicled by Todd Gitlin in *Inside Prime Time* (1983).

It was not its overall ratings, but its segment appeal that saved it. As Seinfeld put it in an interview:

> What made us develop was, despite being very low rated in the beginning, we had a very high demographic profile. Though we were technically bombing, the people watching were what they call advertiser desirable. (Gattuso 1998: 27)

A change in scheduling, however, was to make the real difference to the fortunes of the show. In February 1993, *Seinfeld* was shifted from Wednesday 9.00pm into the attractive Thursdays 9.30pm slot, immediately after *Cheers*. The *Cheers* lead-in made all the difference to the show, improving its audience share by over 50 per cent. Since then, *Seinfeld* was consistently among the top five in the ratings. When *Cheers* went off the air that same year, *Seinfeld* became NBC's Thursday night anchor, subsequently providing a powerful lead-in for another single-in-the-city sitcom, *Friends* in 1994 and 95. At the end of the 1995–96 season Larry David left the show. In the following season, the stand-up intro and exit routines were abandoned, making more time for increasingly intricate and wacky storylines. At the same time, the life of the show was threatened by a dispute between NBC and the three non-owning actors, Alexander, Louis-Dreyfus and Richards, who felt that they were not getting any benefits from the huge profits the show was raking in in syndication – in 1997, Jerry Seinfeld, as creator-producer and actor, was listed by Forbes magazine as having a gross income of $94 million, making him the sixth wealthiest entertainer, whereas the other three of the foursome were making a measly $150,000 per episode. There was a settlement, quadrupling their pay, but they were only to enjoy the fruits of it for one more season (Gattuso 1998: 41–43). At the end of 1997 Jerry Seinfeld decided that the 97–98 season would be the last one – he wanted to go out with a bang while the show was still at its peak, rather than keep on milking the success with a show creatively on the wane, as was perceived to have been the case with shows such as *Family Ties* (1982–89) and *Cheers* (1982–93). The final episode, massively publicized, was aired on 14th May 1998, to an audience of Super Bowl proportions, appropriately written by Larry David. The media frenzy went beyond anything hitherto associated with the ending of a TV comedy series – including the much-hyped finales of *M.A.S.H.* and *Cheers*. The final show itself deserves a few comments.

In this episode the foursome are stranded in a small town and are passive witnesses to the mugging of a fat man. Instead of coming to his assistance, they crack jokes. George: "He's actually doing him a favor. There's less money for him to buy food." They are then arrested by a local police officer and charged with breaking the local 'good Samaritan law' which makes it punishable to refuse to come to the aid of a person in danger. There is a long trial scene in which the New York Four are confronted with minor characters and guest stars from the previous nine years of the show, appearing as character witnesses against them, making for an ironic summary of the history of the show. Judge Art Vandelay (a name George has been using over the years in his various schemes of deception) sentences the four to a year in jail, which is the last the television audience sees of Jerry, George, Elaine and Kramer. An appropriate ironic send-off to a show which resolutely refused any 'learning' or moral preachifying, but which was always concerned, in its unheroic way, with the ethics of everyday existence. The final episode is given a lengthy philosophico-ethical analysis in one of the numerous publications spawned by the success of the show, called *Seinfeld and Philosophy – A Book about Everything and Nothing* (Irwin 2000).

Seinfeld as situation comedy

Although, in a developmental perspective, situation comedy owes more to television than perhaps any other genre, it is not a specifically televisual form – its roots are in the long history of stage entertainment. What gives it its special place in the history of TV genres is its deliberately perfunctory dramatic form, its sketchiness and its staginess. Played out before a 'live studio audience' (although this feature is sometimes dispensed with), camera movement is restricted by the missing fourth wall – the audience position – and any variation of location and post-production editing is heavily limited. There is very little in terms of significant camera or editing action, of slow motion, of inserts, the whole signifying repertoire of cinematography. The camera action is unobtrusive, representing rather than constructing characters in action. Although the gestural dimension is in evidence (witness Kramer), it is essentially dialogue-driven. The fictionality of situation comedy, unlike the major dramatic genres of comedy and tragedy, is perfunctory. The diegesis or story world of sitcom is not a self-contained cocoon. Rather, it insists on its potential openness to 'the real world' – that is the audience world – it is – at least in principle – interruptible by the audience, and its delivery is paced by the audience response. Its interest is not in the far away or the long ago – it is overwhelmingly contemporary.

Seinfeld makes innovative use of these features of sitcom. The presence of Jerry Seinfeld as 'Jerry Seinfeld' is a feature deliberately puncturing the fictionality of representation. As Larry David has put it: "We try to keep Jerry and Jerry as close as we can. We don't want him to do too much acting" (Gattuso, p.101). Indeed, in 'The Pilot', the outrageously metafictional episode in which Jerry and George try to sell the idea of the show 'Jerry – A Show about Nothing' (which is, of course, *Seinfeld*) to NBC, Jerry objects to playing the lead: "I can't act. I stink!" The frequent presence of 'real people' – Keith Hernandez, the baseball player, George Steinbrenner, manager of the New York Yankees and, for a while, George's boss (actually an actor, always shot from behind, with the voice of Larry David) and a host of celebrity cameo appearances – is known from other sitcoms, but adds a continuous sense of permeability with the real contemporary world. (Interestingly, Larry David took the 'anti-fictionality' idea one step further in 1989–90, when he created the HBO comedy series *Curb Your Enthusiasm* with himself in the main role as himself, of Seinfeld fame, and using a mix of actors and celebrities playing themselves.) Add to this the many ways in which the show generates celebrity in anything it touches. The character on which 'The Soup Nazi' is based, the proprietor of Soup Kitchen International at 259-A West 55th Street in New York, a chef known for his outstanding soups and strict queuing discipline is now appearing in a food show on a home-shopping cable channel. The character on which Kramer is loosely based – his name is Kenny Kramer – now makes a living organizing 'Kramer's Reality Tour'– a guided bus tour around sites in New York related to the *Seinfeld* show. And the man who insists on being the real-life George (his name is Mike Costanza) – has tried to capitalize on the success of the show by publishing his autobiography.

The relatively short production time of *Seinfeld* – a week – affords an opportunity of topicality and reference to current events impossible with more cumbersome fictional forms. In the episode 'The Non-Fat Yogurt', a cameo of Rudolph Giuliani, campaigning against fake low-fat yoghurt, was edited into a show hours after Giuliani had won the mayoral election in New York in 1993 and aired the following night.

The narrative of *Seinfeld* is deceptively simple. The half-hour two-act format – with Jerry's intro and exit stand-up routines, the predominance of two locations – Jerry's living room with the couch facing the audience and the booth at Monk's Diner, make for a minimalist setting in which dialogue is foregrounded. There is usually a storyline attached to each of the four characters, sometimes two characters share a storyline. It is, however, as pointed out by Peter Mehlman, one of the scriptwriters, the situations that generate the comedy rather than witty dialogue in itself. As he puts it, "...there are no jokes in the show". And the weaving of storylines into an intricate pattern of often fateful convergence, a well-established sitcom mode of construction, is taken to new and absurd lengths in *Seinfeld*. A supreme example is the episode 'the Pez Dispenser' (January 1992), in which the minute container of candy is the motif and engine of plot convergence.

Intertextuality and metafictionality are frequent features of narrative constructedness in *Seinfeld*. In 'The Boyfriend' (February 1992), a spitting episode during a baseball game is reconstructed in infinitesimal detail, mimicking the investigation into the 1963 assassination of President Kennedy in Dallas. In 'The Betrayal' (November 1997), the backward temporal structure of Harold Pinter's play *Betrayal* from 1978 is borrowed, lending a mock – or perhaps not so mock – philosophical perspective to the episode, with suggestions of the unpredictable consequences of human actions and the irreversibility of time. And, as referred to already, the self-reflexive/metafictional *jeux d'esprit* of selling the 'reality-based' show 'Jerry' to NBC is a thread through several episodes, concluding in an hour-long episode, 'The Pilot', complete with casting interviews for lookalikes playing George, Elaine and Kramer – in fact, Kramer auditions for, and wins, the role as 'himself'.

Seinfeld – 'The show about nothing'

The basic unit of television is not the show but the series, which gives television an advantage in building character over every other narrative medium except perhaps the novel saga. This is also why television is not so much a medium of stories as of moods and atmosphere. We tune in not to find out what is happening (for generally the same things are always happening) but to spend time with characters. In the

1990's *Seinfeld* was promoted as a show 'about nothing' – as if that were unique. All sitcoms are about 'nothing' – nothing but character. (Monaco 2000: 488)

The point made above by James Monaco is well taken. We do tune in to sitcoms to spend time in the company of increasingly familiar characters. But Monaco's comment is also wide of the mark. Sitcoms – including *Seinfeld* – are not about character, hence, about nothing. Sitcoms – like all drama – in Aristotelian terminology – are about character *in action*, and the impetus of action – like all drama – is provided by situations producing dilemmas or conflicts. What is special about Seinfeld is the way in which it deliberately foregrounds the quotidian nature of its dilemmas – its everydayness. The show's casting itself as 'a show about nothing' is a promotional strategy for profiling difference in the marketplace of sitcoms, as a sitcom of resolute minimalism. It does not want to present itself as edifying, and it does not want to present itself as empathetic. As Larry David puts it: "No hugging, no learning" (Irwin 2000: 183). Or, as formulated by Peter Mehlman: "99% of the world is on the verge of tears, what's the big deal to push them over?" (Mehlman 1994) The show may be said to be postmodernist, not only because of its preoccupation with metafictionality, intertextuality and self-reflexivity – buzzwords of the postmodernist – but equally, and perhaps more importantly, because there is no agenda, no explicit or implicit allegiance to the grand emancipatory or ameliorative narratives of modernism. Of course, comedy was never a problem-solving genre. Its business was always to point to incongruities, between preaching and practice, between the size of problems and our attention to them, between the grotesque consequences of minute actions. Comedic resolutions, as Northrop Frye has taught us, were always imposed, magical, arbitrary, in Shakespeare and elsewhere. One of the most controversial episodes of *Seinfeld* – 'The Invitations' – the last episode Larry David wrote before he left the show at the end of the 1995–96 season – makes that point eloquently. In the episode, George is desperate to free himself from the commitment to marry Susan. The *deus ex machina* is provided by the toxic glue on the cheap envelopes of the marriage invitations, the licking of which produces the death of Susan, to the poorly concealed relief of George, who is quick to follow up on his secret infatuation with actress Marisa Tomei. As Gattuso puts it,

The episode divided fans, who were either floored by the intensity of David's black comedy or outraged that the series' sole likable character – one whose flaw was her taste in men – was killed off so unceremoniously. [...] Despite the flood of angry phone calls fielded by NBC switchboards, the *Seinfeld* team got a good chuckle and one of its highest ratings ever. (Gattuso 1998: 33)

Judging by the audience response, this episode did 'push the envelope' of the genre of the sitcom, even as determined by the expectations of the otherwise magnanimous *Seinfeld* audience. Yet, the ambition of Seinfeld and David was always to delve into areas beyond, or beneath, the attention of mainstream network sitcoms. The examples are legion. A much discussed episode was 'The Contest' (November 1992), in which the four characters make a wager about who will abstain the longest from masturbation –

(the word was never used during the episode), implicitly establishing masturbation as a natural phenomenon among singles. Another episode is 'The Outing' (February 1993), in which a newspaper publishes rumours about Jerry and George being lovers. The ambiguity of their scandalized reaction combined with their liberal lip service to the acceptability of homosexuality produced one of the catchphrases of the 90s: 'Not that there is anything wrong with that'. The episode won the show a media award from the Gay and Lesbian Alliance Against Defamation.

What is the special appeal of a show such as *Seinfeld*? Audience figures and recurrent media debates are quantifiable ways of documenting the purchase it has had on public opinion. Its afterlife in syndication worldwide ensures its position as a popular cultural icon of the 1990s. However, if one looks more closely at the specific ways it has impacted with its audience, it is without doubt the particular conversational idiom of the show which accounts its major appeal. Hundreds of personal websites testify to this. Its roots in stand-up comedy, with its knack of turning the minutiae of everyday life dilemmas into philosophical conundrums, gave the show an immediacy of appeal which went far beyond the set-up/pay-off dominated structure of previous sitcoms. It is a paradox of its appeal that however much it refused to cater to identification and character empathy, the show was overwhelmingly perceived to reflect its audience's idioms and concerns. The way in which a whole range of expressions and catchphrases have entered contemporary American testifies to this: 'Yada', 'Not that there is anything wrong with it', 'get out', 'shrinkage' – the list goes on and on. This is not simply a testimony to the extraordinary economical skills of the scriptwriters associated with the show, but just as much an effect of the exceptional authorial control Larry David and Jerry Seinfeld wielded on it. *Seinfeld*, for all its laid-back conversational casualness, is – paradoxically – an unusually *auteured* sitcom. Over its nine years of production, for all its variety of themes and narrative structures, it has maintained a consistency of approach to the basic ingredients of its own project – a philosophical minimalist conversationalism, an acute sense of the dynamics of ordinary contemporary idiom and a ruthless honesty in the exploration of the everyday anxieties of post-adolescent urban singledom.

Seinfeld, *Friends*, *Ally McBeal* etc. – looking for a paradigm
It is obvious that shows such as *Seinfeld*, *Friends* and *Ally McBeal* are riding the same wave of network orientation towards a particular audience segment: 18–49's in general, more specifically urban singles. As Gattuso has it:

> The success of *Seinfeld* has made a cottage industry out of the adult-oriented, single-in-the-city sitcoms. The exception to the 'singles' rule was NBC's *Mad about You*, with Paul Reiser as essentially a married Jerry Seinfeld. NBC created *Friends*, which got a Seinfeldian billing by the network as 'A new comedy about...whatever'. Most recently, NBC launched *Caroline in the City* and *The Single Guy* on Thursday night to attract the *Seinfeld/Friends* crowd. ABC's *Ellen* and Fox's *Living Single* are spun from similar threads. (Gattuso 1998: 29)

To this could be added HBO's extraordinarily successful and raunchy chick show, *Sex and the City* (1998–2004).

There are solid demographic as well as narrative reasons for the success of this genre. More than half of all adult Americans now live in 'single households'. Because of the purchasing power of this audience segment, shows appealing to them are interesting vehicles for advertisers. In addition, narratively speaking, young adult singles are the very stuff of which fiction is made. The history of the novel, from Jane Austen onwards, is testimony to the narrative dynamics of the 'not yet married'. They are, as it were, a romance waiting to happen. Their transitional position between adolescence and their social ensconcement within the societal bastions of career, procreation and marriage is guaranteed to invoke themes of existential anxiety with a wide identificatory appeal. Furthermore, within the paradigm there is plenty of scope for variation. Along gender lines, *Seinfeld*, *Friends* and *Ally McBeal* provide a neat distribution of focus. *Seinfeld* is primarily male-oriented, with Elaine as 'one of the boys'. As Kramer tells her in 'The Pool Guy': "You're a man's woman – you hate other women and they hate you". *Friends* is precisely balanced in terms of male/female interest. *Ally McBeal* has an overwhelmingly female focus. This mirrors a parallel distribution along an axis of, at one end, ironic detachment and at the other end empathetic sentiment, with *Seinfeld* at the ironic end, *Ally McBeal* at the other end, tending towards melodrama, and *Friends* somewhere in the middle (given to unevenness of scriptwriting), toying with the ambiguities of the ironic and the empathetic.

Are these shows postmodern? The question raises a host of issues which reach far beyond the scope of this paper. From an aesthetic point of view, the application of the usual buzzwords 'intertextuality', 'self-reflexivity', 'metafictionality' will distribute the three shows along an axis placing *Ally McBeal* as very PM, *Seinfeld* as fairly PM, and *Friends* as not very PM. If however, one opts for a broader socio-psychological approach, which situates the 'world picture' of the shows within the vocabulary of sociological criticism from Lasch to Giddens and Ulrich Beck, applying such terms as 'narcissism', 'individualization', 'decline of metanarratives', 'unhookedness', 'risk society' etc., there seems to be a broader sense of uniformity across the range of the chosen television 'texts'. It is, however, a sense of shared concerns which is deceptive, in the sense that an analysis should not lose sight of the extraordinary variety of textual strategies in the face of those shared concerns. Nor should any analysis of any television content lose sight of the specificities and constraints of cultural production. As Jim Collins puts it in his essay 'Television and Postmodernism', in an argument with Fredric Jameson's position of the postmodern as the superstructure of late capitalism:

> The problem for television studies, as it tries to come to terms with postmodernism, is how to reconcile the semiotic and economic dimensions of television. Stressing the semiotic to the exclusion of the economic produces only a formalist game of 'let's count the intertexts', but privileging the economic to the point that semiotic complexity is reduced to a limited set of moves allowed by a master system is just as

simplistic. The attempt to turn television into a master system operating according to a single logic is a fundamentally nostalgic perspective; the culture of the 1990's, though judged to be the sheer noise of late capitalism, is nevertheless expected to operate according to nineteenth-century models of culture as homogeneous totality. (Collins 2000: 766)

Pierson's point, cited in the opening paragraph of this essay, about sitcoms as contemporary comedies of manners, is well taken, and I would argue that *Seinfeld* is a particularly salient case in point. The argument above made by Collins about the semiotic and economic dimensions of television studies could be applied to the everyday games played by all of us and mirrored, in an extreme and stylized form, in sitcoms such as *Seinfeld*. Culture, I would agree with Collins, should not be viewed as a 'homogeneous totality' with our individual selves as 'Träger'. Rather, as mirrored by TV comedies in general and sitcoms such as *Seinfeld* in particular, culture is a complex of ongoing negotiations concerning the definitions of 'civility', i.e. the practical ethics among friends, lovers, within families, at the workplace and as citizens. Shows like *Seinfeld* may come to an end, as their specific narrative repertoires are depleted, but the well of the human comedy of manners will never run dry – Not That There's Anything Wrong With That!

References

Attalah, Paul, 1984: 'The Unworthy Discourse – Situation Comedy in Television', in *Interpreting Television: Current Research Perspectives*, Willard D. Rowland, Jr and Bruce Watkin (eds), Sage Annual Reviews of Communication Research vol.12.

Bryant, John, 1979: 'Emma, Lucy and the American Situation Comedy of Manners' *Journal of Popular Culture* vol. 13, no. 2, Autumn, pp. 248–56.

Collins, Jim, 2000: 'Television and Postmodernism', in Stam, Robert and Miller, Toby, eds., *Film and Theory – An Anthology*, Blackwell.

Curtis, Barry, 1982: 'Aspects of Sitcom', in *Television Sitcom*, BFI Dossier 17, British Film Institute.

David, Larry and Seinfeld, Jerry, 1998: *The Seinfeld Scripts – The First and Second Seasons*, Castle Rock Entertainment.

Gattuso, Greg, 1988: *The Seinfeld Universe: The Entire Domain*, BBC.

Gitlin, Todd, 1983: *Inside Prime Time*, New York, Pantheon.

Hough, Arthur, 1986: 'Trials and Tribulations – Thirty Years of Sitcom', in *Understanding Television*, ed. by Richard P. Adler, Praeger.

Irwin William, (ed.), 2000: *Seinfeld and Philosophy – A Book about Everything and Nothing*, Chicago, Opencourt.

Johnson, Carla, 1994: 'Luckless in New York: The Schlemiel and the Schlimazl in Seinfeld', *Journal of Popular Film and Television* vol. 22, no. 3, Autumn, pp. 116–24.

Lasch, Christopher, 1980: *The Culture of Narcissism*, London, Abacus.

McConnell, Frank, 1996: 'How *Seinfeld* Was Born: Jane Austen Meets Woody Allen' *Commonwealth* vol. 123, no. 3, 9 February, pp. 19–20.

Mehlman, Peter, 1994: *Writing Seinfeld-Style*, Writer's Audio Shop, 90 mins.

Monaco, James, 2000: *How To Read A Film*, 3rd edition, Oxford University Press.

Pierson, David P., 2000: 'A Show about Nothing: *Seinfeld* and the Modern Comedy of Manners', *Journal of Popular Culture* vol. 34, no. 1, Summer, pp. 49–64.

Seinfeld, Jerry, 1993: *Seinlanguage*, Bantam Books, New York.

Seinfeld, Jerry et al., 1999: *Sein Off – The Final Days of Seinfeld*, London, Boxtree, (orig. pub. 1998).

Television's Vanishing Terms? Traditional Aesthetics and Television Drama in the Age of Reality TV

Felix Thompson

Can television criticism be said to have changed its ground in response to the age of reality television? The sense that such a shift has taken place can be illustrated by two books published in recent years. John Caughie's *Television Drama – Realism, Modernism and British Culture*, published in 2000, is based on his writings since the 1970s. It looks back to the aesthetic debates of the 1960s and 70s in a period of few television channels and the high profile of a public service remit. In the circumstances of tensions around the post-Second World War social democratic settlement,[1] television drama is to be interrogated through what might be called traditional aesthetics – debates about realism and naturalism as predominant modes and modernism as an alternative. The touchstones here in terms of literary and dramatic theory are the work of Lukacs, Brecht and Bakhtin. In addition, the book figures those who straddled the divide between the 'traditional' aesthetic debates of high modernism and contemporary cultural theory – Adorno, Horkheimer and Raymond Williams. It is only the latter, though, who makes an appearance in the collection *Understanding Reality Television* edited by Su Holmes and Deborah Jermyn published four years later and, in this case, solely for his pioneering exploration of television form rather than, for instance, his extensive exploration of the boundaries and intersections between realism, naturalism and modernism. Instead, in the more recent collection, the touchstones are drawn from contemporary cultural studies, figures who, in general, would not deal in traditional aesthetic categories associated with textual form – Bourdieu, McRobbie, Scannell and Richard Dyer. To be sure, the emphasis is going to be different for a book dealing with factual television rather than television drama, but does this mean that there should also be a shift away from traditional aesthetics when we are dealing with television drama?

The sense that a shift is required in the critical discourses appropriate to the discussion of television drama may be traced to the major change in the competitive climate in which television drama is produced and the rise of the kind of values associated with 'reality' television. The debate about television drama before 1990 developed when television was restricted to broadcasting on only a few channels, each able to secure a large segment of the audience and a relatively stable stream of funding for drama production. In a less competitive climate, each channel was able to claim some level of commitment to public service values associated with the interests of the community. The change from public service values to a market-driven, multi-channel context – in which securing as much of the fragmented audience as possible becomes paramount – is often summed up as a change from address to the citizen to address to the consumer. This is a shift from more collective values to the promotion of individualism, although what the individualism of the consumer being addressed actually means in the context of television drama is something which requires investigation.

The debate about the meaning of reality television can be seen as emblematic of these changes. John Corner, in summarizing the diverse phenomena which are represented by the term 'reality TV, notes the industrial connection between the proliferation of television channels in the 1990s and the requirement for cheap programming in a period of intensified competition. This is accompanied by the increasing preoccupation of the factual programming of television with everyday private experience, a desire to be inside that experience and the emotional knowledge associated with it (Corner 2004: 291). It is striking, though, that what seems to be being described is territory already occupied by fictional drama. The ascent of reality TV seems to be part of a development which has often been claimed for the disappearance of the boundary between the factual and the fictional.[2]

Yet in reviewing *This Life* (BBC2, 1996–97) and *Queer as Folk* (Channel 4, 1999–2000), two notable series of the 1990s appearing in the midst of the kind of industrial shifts described by Corner, it is intended here to argue a rather different case – that television drama continues to have significant marks of difference from the developments represented by reality television. This is partly because television drama is a broad stream in which change has been incremental rather than wholesale, with a considerable degree of continuity of practice in soap operas, dramas based on public services or authored drama. But *This Life* and *Queer as Folk* could be seen as the kind of lifestyle dramas with a kinship to some of the most high-profile examples of reality TV. It is in exploring the possibility of such a kinship that I will argue nevertheless that a significant divergence emerges. This divergence relates to the way in which these television dramas are still haunted by the aesthetic modes of naturalism and melodrama which speak in different ways of continuing anxieties about the contemporary social formation even if it is pervaded by an individualist consumer ethic. In particular, here, it is important to recognize the implications of these aesthetic modes as they became embedded within television from their longer history within literature and drama, implications arising from an extended encounter with the vicissitudes of modernity since the nineteenth century. This will be to suggest then that the apparently vanishing terms of traditional aesthetics are still meaningful in the age of reality television.

Drama and scarcity

John Ellis has recently suggested that, during the twentieth century, television evolved through successive phases of scarcity, availability and plenty. This evolution refers in his argument to the development from a single channel in the middle of the last century to the multi-channel saturation of the 1990s and is connected to a concomitant or parallel proliferation of consumer choice in general. The period of scarcity of the television image is associated with a drive for 'universal provision' in which television was regarded as akin to a public utility on a par with the refrigerator (Ellis 2002: 40). In Ellis's third era, in a situation of plenty, choice in the possible outcomes of narrative is firmly linked to the idea of intensified consumerism (Ellis, 2002: 76). Choice through television becomes a multiplicity of options or frameworks for viewing the world:

> At the same time as a news story breaks about a racially motivated murder, for example, there will already be various other kinds of programming dealing with the issue of race and racism in various ways. Characters in soap operas will be confronting prejudice; comedy programmes like *Goodness Gracious Me* will be lampooning reverse racism; documentaries will be examining particular issues; the black newsreader Trevor McDonald will be voted the most trusted man in Britain; and Rory Bremner will be using him as material for a satire on the tendency of news to adopt the forms of entertainment television. (Ellis: 79)

As Ellis himself notes, though, this is a situation of 'uneven development' in which parts of the old ways of viewing continue in the present (Ellis: 162). In the case of drama, Ellis concentrates on distinctions between series, serial and the single play or upon the open-ended nature of much television drama within a multiplicity of possible narratives. It is to be suggested here that there was a further dimension of uneven development in the way that television absorbed many of the forms and aesthetic modes from pre-televisual history. Television drama deploys key aesthetic modes originally associated with the theatre and literature, which speak of an extended history of scarcity and social conflict before the consumer age. In the evolution of television criticism these practices, described by terms such as naturalism, realism, modernism and melodrama, were key areas of contention in debates about television's adequacy to the universal democratic aspirations of its audience.

The application of these terms in television criticism has been in itself rather uneven though. Caughie's book, for instance, centres on major disputes about the practices of naturalism, realism and modernism in the traditions of authored drama from the 1960s to the 1980s but has little mention of melodrama. By contrast, in her book *Women and*

Soap Opera, Christine Geraghty considered the operation of the everyday realism of soaps in a hybrid with elements of melodrama (Geraghty 1990).[3] Geraghty's work makes a notable advance by asking how different aesthetic modes work together but, unsurprisingly in the context of soap operas, she doesn't discuss modernism. Like Geraghty, Caughie also advances beyond traditional aesthetics, in this case through an engagement with Bakhtin which leads to his discussion of the television text as novelistic. The novelistic in television is associated with a pattern of interruptability, a constantly changing point of view arising from a pattern of mutual interruption between the short segments that constitute the basis of television form and between discourses and genres. Such an argument lays the basis here for assessing the radical intersection of diverse aesthetic modes in television and just as importantly for making sense of television as a hybrid text. If we are to make sense of the vestiges of traditional aesthetic modes within the contemporary hybrid television text we will have to expect them to become manifest only in brief snatches within a pattern of interruption. For instance, melodrama may only be present through allusions to the possibility of moral polarization, emotional expressiveness and the symbolic deployment of family archetypes.[4] Equally, naturalist observation of the effects of social and physical environment upon character may only be transitory and not sustained. The associated social democratic interest in using the naturalist mode to delineate a social problem and suggest the need, if not the means for its amelioration, may only be hinted at. The social issue for instance may be suggested then set aside by a desire to identify more closely with the pleasures of the characters or to enjoy the more unexpected turns of a dramatic fiction.

It is being suggested here that to invoke either melodrama or naturalism – or just as likely their intersection – in the contemporary television text is to hark back to conditions of scarcity. While melodrama has been used often enough to register the effects of material scarcity, the major fear to which the emotions are most significantly attached is that of a failure in the symbolization of family relations. The scarcity which is of concern here is the lack of options within archetypal family relationships. To harp on this through the nineteenth century and much of the twentieth has often been a means to explore the adequacy of the relations of gender or sexuality. There are recurrent junctures in a contemporary television drama where the expressiveness and polarization of melodrama may be invoked for the same reasons. Material scarcity may have been replaced by consumer plenty but this does not mean that there is a necessary expansion in choice of relationships, especially if they are to carry an emotionally rewarding symbolic value. On the other hand, in the age of reality television, amongst suggestions of the possibility of achieving identity through consumer choice and personal self-fashioning, the vision of the morally polarized world of melodrama may become too restrictive and limiting.

The scarcity associated with naturalism is of the much more observable material kind although it may be fairly obviously mediated through social and family relationships (hence, a tendency within naturalist dramas to shade into the expressiveness of melodrama). In the situation described by John Ellis, in the first period of television's development of the realization of universal provision, provision or failure to provide was seen as the responsibility of the social democratic state. Not surprisingly many of the most famous examples of naturalist television drama dealing with issues of universal provision focused on the workings of the welfare state in the postwar years.[5] Essential to the documentation of failures of universal provision was the use of an apparently neutral public gaze.[6] Subjective involvement with protagonists must be limited by the requirement to observe from a distance how they were affected by environmental and social conditions.

But it must also be recognized that television offered another version of the naturalist observational gaze which could, for instance, sustain the everyday realism of soap operas. In this case there would be no necessary connection with any particular social issue or social problem. As David Buckingham argued concerning the early years of *EastEnders* (BBC1, 1985–), while a long list of social issues were present implicitly, the need for dramatic conflict and entertainment had to prevail (Buckingham 1987: 83–4). Social issues too easily risked appearing didactic against the background of such everyday drama and, therefore, their appearance was heavily circumscribed. Furthermore, the everyday gaze of the soap opera also provided a starting point for departure into a more self-consciously performative mode of television. Soaps were one of the key sites where television began to juxtapose what might be called discourses of self-fashioning alongside the observation of the everyday. Thus, writing in 1990, Christine Geraghty's other key element in everyday British soaps is that of light entertainment (Geraghty: 29). In British soaps she notes that there is 'a strong tradition of glamorous middle-aged women'. In this respect she suggest that light entertainment 'looks for an identity between star and character' (Geraghty: 36), suggesting how a dimension of the text projects beyond the fictional world into a wider popular consciousness. The performance of such roles in a non-fictional world, which has recently been strongly associated with reality television, had thus already developed in juxtaposition with more traditional aesthetic modes such as naturalism and melodrama.

Reality Television and contemporary drama in the 1990s

To what extent have these patterns of hybridization evolved as consumer- orientated aspirations become more manifest, for instance, through the changes associated with reality television in the 1990s? I will concentrate here on the heavy emphasis placed on performance of persona in reality television and on the lifestyle that belongs to that persona. As John Corner notes of *Big Brother*, 'living space is also performance space' (Corner 2002: 257).[7] The concern with lifestyle and persona is very much attached to the possibility of transformation. What this adds up to is the possibility of self-fashioning which will allow the performer to escape from the historical determinations of the past. As Thomas Sutcliffe puts it in relation to makeover programmes 'there is an almost seamless diet of improvement...an implicit promise that everything is getting better'.[8] Rachel Moseley describes how the series *Shopping City* (BBC1/BBC2, 1999–2000) actually combines docusoap with makeover by following a group of people making shopping choices. It exemplifies how the public service role of television has become consumer centred, encouraging self-improvement by teaching how to shop 'more efficiently' (Moseley 2000: 301). Ultimately this allows aspiration to celebrity status. Thus, as Moseley notes, *Stars in their Eyes* (ITV, 1990–) starts with the ordinary person in their everyday routine and shows the process of conversion into their chosen performer (Moseley: 308).

Similarly, the notion of a contest winner in game format 'reality' shows or media recognition of 'successful' personalities in docusoaps hold out the possibility of personal transformation and, indeed, celebrity. But, in addition in these cases, a similarity to the complications of fictional drama may be apparent in the complex relationships and plots which build up in docusoaps and the game format shows. John Corner notes in the context of *Big Brother*:

> Social cohesion, personality, and capacity to perform tasks can be variously emphasised within combinations of the instructive and entertaining. The 'self' can be put on display in various modes of affection, solidarity, insincerity, confrontation and downright aggression...

> Participant self-reflection and commentary can deepen the plots thrown up by interaction. Self-knowledge can strengthen viewer empathy, while 'self-ignorance' (along with its partner, over confidence) holds, as ever, its classic potential for comic effect. (Corner, 2002: 261)

As part of this process, one notable feature is the role of the confessional asides or 'participant testimony' (Corner: 257) to the viewer in which a participant reviews their position within the ongoing struggle for transformation. Thus, as in drama, we may be given the perspective of each participant. Corner speaks of a process of 'selving' in *Big Brother*:

> A certain amount of the humdrum and the routine may be a necessary element in giving this selving process, this *unwitting* disclosure of the personal core, its measure of plausibility, aligning it with the mundane rhythms and naturalistic portrayals of docusoap, soap opera itself, and, at times, the registers of game show participation. (Corner: 262)

Is, though, the process of 'selving' in fictional drama actually like this? The two dramas chosen here from the 1990s both place the role of 'selving', of the presentation of an appropriate persona amongst a group of young people at their centre. Both *This Life* and *Queer as Folk* are principally concerned with young adults who see each other on a regular basis to the extent that they form a sense of community or at least an in-group. Both series were aimed at capturing newer and younger audiences by 'pushing boundaries'.[9] Like *Big Brother* (Channel 4, 2000–) subsequently and earlier docusoaps of the 1990s such as *The Living Soap* (BBC, 1993–94), they also include participant testimony, spoken straight to camera, which allows characters to comment on their place within the drama. This has the effect of opening up the options about how they should behave, about the problems they may face in taking a particular course in the light of the behaviour of others and their feelings towards others. The particular age range of the central characters also opens up the realms of possibility in terms of their choices in life.

In the case of *This Life* the central household, mainly composed of lawyers, is 'somewhere between obedience and responsibility, final exams and the mortgage' (Sutcliffe: 24). Although legal cases figure from their day jobs, they are used to illustrate issues of character or explored in their effect on relationships between characters within the household. No actual scenes are shown in court and, instead, there are numerous scenes of mealtimes, interactions between characters at home and in the workplace, parties, pubs, sexual encounters and incidental drug taking. The restrictions of work are broadly shown as barriers to the freedom and hedonism which is presented as the main goal of young people before the stage of commitment. Placed on the boundary line between freedom and commitment there are many moments in the two series when the characters' behaviour is presented as quite unpredictable and in some cases openly transgressive. Thus, Egg's choices after he drops out of his legal career range from becoming a novelist to running a restaurant. The high flier, Miles, from a public school background, becomes besotted with Delilah who is simply taking him for a ride on behalf of her drug-dealing lover. The hard-working Milly, who is the most committed to her work and her long-standing relationship with Egg, starts an affair with her boss. The whole notion of respectability in terms of the middle-class codes of the legal profession to which they aspire is also brought into question in the first series through the gay character, Warren, who brings home people he has picked up with different backgrounds and social aspirations.

The visual style at first appears very much to belong to that of the observational camera – unsteady, hand-held, often long-lens short glimpses of characters across rooms. Yet the jerkiness goes beyond the kind of unpredictable camera movement that suggests observed spontaneous action, often shading into a detached mannerism. Nick Halsted associates this 'twitchy' style with the unpredictability of the narrative, "avoiding happy endings and, sometimes, any endings at all" (Halsted: 6). In a sense this is a part of the prospectus of the series to present narratives which are not yet fixed in their consequences because they arise amongst a group of young people who are supposedly free from conventional restrictions. While there is no resemblance in visual style to subsequent game-format reality TV such as *Big Brother*, the claim that nothing is fixed for the characters at the beginning of the narrative is significant. Just as at the beginning of *Big Brother*, we start with a group of young people for whom everything is up for grabs. There are all the elements of 'selving' which Corner discusses. We can believe that these characters are in the act of making who they are. *This Life* appears to be a drama of self-fashioning which belongs to the developing consumer orientation of the 1990s, calculated as it was to bring in the young audience, the rising consumers.

In terms of traditional aesthetics, then, it would appear that the stark moral dilemmas allowed by melodrama are not relevant. Equally a drama of self-fashioning would avoid suggesting that these characters are driven by social forces which they cannot resist, as we might expect from naturalism. However, closer inspection of particular episodes and storylines shows that the aesthetic modes of melodrama and naturalism and the associated issues of scarcity are significantly present. This may be best illustrated by the story of Miles' 'girlfriend' Delilah in episodes 2, 3 and 4 of the first series. Delilah is first encountered by Anna and Miles outside a court hearing in which she is to be a witness for a young man, Truelove, with whom she shares a house. In the circumstances of the court she is presented as someone who belongs to the realm of clients and social problems. Anna observes that she is 'on drugs' – but she differentiates this from the hedonism of their circle of friends who confine their drug habits to the weekend. In keeping with the suggestion that these characters can avoid traditional middle-class destinies, Miles responds to sexual advances from Delilah and begins a relationship with her. She moves into the house with him, bringing a television which the rest of the household do not want. It emerges that she is bulimic and otherwise unstable. Her claims to be following a career in modelling are fantasy and other members of the household show obvious disdain for her. Above all she has not broken off her relationship with Truelove. Her theft of possessions from members of the household on Truelove's behalf and the subsequent revelation that Truelove is a heroin addict ultimately demonstrates that Delilah and her real boyfriend come from a world other than young university-educated twenty-somethings at the beginning of their careers.

The significance of this storyline is that Delilah and Truelove belong to a world in which they cannot control their own destinies or make their own choices. Their personality defects and appetite for drugs mean that they are unable to accumulate enough money to live a pleasure-seeking life without getting into debt to loan sharks or resorting to theft. They are sharply differentiated from the lawyers' household by allowing their transgressions to extend to property rights and by allowing their hedonism to become uncontrollably destructive. In this respect they belong to a pattern which has been common in literary naturalism since the nineteenth century. David Baguley describes this as the pathetic tragic decline of a central character – often a voyeuristic replay of the fallen woman myth, a fascination with feminine pathology as a source of chaos (Baguley 1990: 103). Such characters are shown to be pulled down by the determinist effects of bad heredity and ultimately swallowed by a dehumanized environment (Baguley: 82). In this case, similarly, Delilah and her real boyfriend provide the spectre of a social world determined by inadequate personality and, indeed, the contamination of disease. It is Warren, the gay member of the household, who is first to fully comprehend what Delilah really is. When she disappears he leads Miles to Truelove's lodgings. Not only does the absence of furniture indicate a degraded state but the scene is lit by a low central light which throws shadows across faces and against the walls behind the actors. The sense of possible evil and destructive forces which might be associated with melodrama is defused though by the calm rationality of Warren who insists that HIV tests should be carried out to assess the real risk, allowing Miles to establish that he is free of contamination. In this respect the central characters (as opposed to Delilah and Truelove) can skirt around a melodramatically heightened threat to their existence (as might be suggested by the lighting) and remain in control of their own hedonism and their career path of self-creation in the rest of the drama. It is the continued maintenance of such an openness to possibility, as against the tropes of scarcity indicated by such episodes as Miles' relationship with Delilah, that becomes the main theme of the drama over two series and twenty-one episodes.

Central to such openness is the figure of Anna who defines her outlook by stating, "I don't want a boyfriend, I want a fuck". This outlook is constantly tested through the series as her continued physical desire for Miles threatens a conventionality which she is trying to avoid. Her progress in self-fashioning is also tested through a seeming problem with alcohol and drug abuse. It almost seems she will crack up, especially after failing to go to her mother's funeral. But she steadfastly resists Miles' ultimate fate as he succumbs to a relationship and a wedding which, symbolically at least, exclude him from the hedonistic plenty which Anna is still free to pursue. The frequent scenes of Anna, darkly lit at night-time in a state of nervous tension or personal inner conflict, indicate the cost of the path she has taken as she continues to shrug off the consequences of making choices which avoid becoming tied down by conventional expectations. The lighting is often potentially melodramatic but her actions defy the limited set of binary choices associated with melodrama. If *This Life* is a lifestyle drama, then, it is one in which there is a thematization of the possibilities and costs of self-fashioning. The costs and risks of scarcity are figured here through the vestigial tropes of naturalism and melodrama.

Critical identification of these tropes of scarcity in material or emotional form is, then, an aid to understanding the way in which this drama cannot entirely escape anxieties of the past. This can also be seen amidst the even greater commitment to hedonism in *Queer as Folk*. Once again here there is a thematization of unfettered self-fashioning in relation to other possibilities. Stuart, the most successful of the group of gay acquaintances in making nightly pick-ups in clubs and pubs, represents the ultimate possibility in single-minded pleasure-seeking. Yet, by contrast, zones occupied by other characters appear to be marked by restriction. Vince, for instance, works as a middle manager in a supermarket where he conceals the fact that he is gay. Nathan, who is still fifteen, must endure the predictable prejudices against his sexuality in school and from parents. Stuart has a lifestyle to which the others aspire. His flat occupies a whole floor in a former warehouse in a district which is apparently devoid of rows of judgmental neighbours which are found in the suburban areas. It is filled with new technology, liberating Stuart from the kind of drudgery such as shelf-filling or school work associated with his friends. The images of gay pornography which he controls on the screens around him amplify the freedom of an apparently infinite series of sexual couplings, so free that it seems a genuine mistake when he tries to pick up someone he has picked up before. The drama ebbs and flows between the two zones as Vince and Nathan try to follow Stuart's example. Vince, for instance, is never quite as successful in his pick-ups.

Even when he does manage it, a long-term relationship evolves. The domesticity of a settled couple is uncomfortable for Vince, though, and meets with Stuart's disdain. Nathan's problems are more straightforward. He lacks the income and the type of residence to fully follow Stuart – but he is beginning to learn.

If the obstacles for Vince and Nathan in following Stuart are illustrated through these shortcomings, then his irruption into the domestic suburban world is equally important. After having sex with the under-age Nathan, Stuart ostentatiously drives him to the front door of his school in a four-wheel drive, defiantly displaying the homophobic graffiti which have been sprayed on the vehicle. When he does something as mundane as visit a car showroom, he test drives the car through the plate glass of the showroom window straight towards the salesman whose homophobic remarks have not been appreciated. His almost demonic role in defending his way of life and encouraging others to follow suit does not form part of any obvious moral scheme within the drama though, his stance and his lifestyle are simultaneously presented as both potentially liberating from the constraints of straight domestic suburbia and potentially destructive. It is in suburbia that the naturalist elements of the drama arise. In visual terms suburbia is flatly lit and drab, forming a strong contrast to the pulsating lights and music of pubs and clubs or the darkly lit streets as a setting for night-time revelry. The school or the home are locations where homophobia from schoolmates or parents can be set up for observation. Nathan is shown being threatened by his unsympathetic father or by other boys in the school. Similarly, Vince must deal with the assumption that he will find one of the young women who workfor him in the supermarket to be attractive. He is shown in an average everyday working environment where homophobia or at least dominant heterosexual assumptions prevail.

It should also be noted then that there is an absence of any kind of energetic investment in the symbolic family relationships associated with melodrama. The nearest the drama comes to this is in an early episode when one of the group dies after taking a bad batch of cocaine. The subsequent funeral, though, is turned into an opportunity for the renewed assertion of the commitment of the group to continue their lifestyle as Stuart begins to look for another pick-up. The only dissenting voice is the mother of the deceased who questions their recklessness. But the hurt in her face is one of simple bereavement and she has no symbolic force. She is just one more voice amongst the general commentary on the lifestyle epitomized by Stuart.

Yet, if there is no symbolic power invested in family relationships in a positive sense there is a drift towards a version of family relationships as a default position, the threat of becoming a sexless, middle-aged couple. Hedonism which escapes the constraints of everyday life is to be undermined by ageing and loss of vitality. The central relationship between Vince and Stuart, which goes back to schooldays, is portrayed as being like that of a married couple. Vince is always hovering on the edge of Stuart's sex life as if he should be involved. But when they finally try to spend the night together there is no desire left. As they approach 30 they can see that the next generation, represented by

Nathan, will take over. This natural force in sex and social relationships is defied only by the fantasy ending of the drama. In the style of the ending of *Grease*, the couple are aerially transported in Stuart's four-wheel drive to a remote road-side café in the Midwest of the USA. Yet this does not convince that they will escape the inexorable fate of domesticity which Stuart is so keen to avoid.

Despite the fantasy ending, *Queer as Folk* sustains, then, an awareness of the pressing-in of apparently natural forces on the characters, whether these forces come from a homophobic environment or the long-term effects of ageing on relationships. This awareness is suggested by maintaining adherence to the kind of discreet observational rhetoric associated with television's everyday naturalism – showing, for instance, an 'average' secondary school or supermarket in which the characters must exist for substantial parts of their lives. This conveys a mundane world where such forces just appear to be naturally there. Possibilities of self-fashioning are hemmed in by a sense of a wider social environment which appears to weigh substantially upon the destiny of the characters. Crucially what it also being indicated is a sense of social space which far exceeds the performance space of individual characters.

During most of its history, naturalism has been traditionally criticized for pessimism in presenting a world in which the fate of characters appears to be determined by social forces.[10] However, that is not quite what is happening in either *Queer as Folk* or *This Life*. Each serial could be said to be presenting a version of the dialogue between, on the one hand, the discourses of selving and personal transformation, most strongly associated with reality TV and, on the other, the sense of limits and socially regulated scarcity, conveyed by certain practices of dramatic fiction. These practices have been described here as traditional aesthetics, in particular naturalism and melodrama. It is, then, through these specific aesthetic modes that anxieties of scarcity are still embedded within the practices of contemporary dramatic fiction and that these fictional worlds can be considered to be set apart from the more wholehearted consumerist individualism associated with large parts of reality TV

In reviewing the kinds of shifts required of television criticism in the age of reality television by such dramas as *This Life* and *Queer as Folk*, the discourses of self-fashioning are, nevertheless, very significant. Through such preoccupations these dramas clearly manifest many of the concerns of reality television itself. A key question, though, is how to make sense of the coexistence of apparently incompatible frameworks – a belief in an unfettered self-fashioning alongside perspectives of restriction and scarcity, indicated by the traditional aesthetic modes of melodrama and naturalism. John Ellis has described this process in which television permutates multiple frameworks and perspectives on the world as a process of 'working through', 'a constant process of making and remaking meanings and of exploring possibilities'. He argues that this is necessary in a situation where television threatens a kind of information overload, without providing a sufficiently stable explanatory framework (Ellis 2000: ibid.). But, equally, television criticism needs to be attentive to a continuing anxiety that multiple frameworks may be closed off and that singular deterministic social forces may be at work. Television criticism in an age of plenty needs to maintain an awareness that television itself still betrays an anxiety about its own discourses of plenty.

Notes

1. The postwar settlement is firmly inscribed in chapter 3, Caughie's discussion of British television's 'golden age' (Caughie 2000).
2. Such arguments can be traced back at least to debates about the hybridization of documentary and drama in the 1980s. These are summed up by Julian Petley who suggests that 'the rigid fact/fiction dichotomy is increasingly being called into question by television itself' (Petley 1996: 19).
3. This argument is also developed by Ien Ang (Ang 1985). David Buckingham notes the movement between naturalism, melodrama and comedy (Buckingham 1985: 75).
4. For full accounts of melodrama from nineteenth-century theatre through the beginnings of cinema to television soap opera, see Brooks (1995) and Gledhill (1987).
5. Exemplified by such dramas as *Cathy Come Home* (BBC, 1966, director Ken Loach, writer Jeremy Sandford).
6. For a discussion of the development of this public gaze in the British context see Higson (1986).
7. In relation to the series *Style Challenge* (BBC 1, 1996–98) 1996 Rachel Moseley talks of the foregrounding of 'the production of gendered self' (Moseley: 305).
8. 'Eye on Friday', *The Independent*, September 1997, p. 3. Quoted by Rachel Moseley, op. cit., p. 300.
9. *This Life* was commissioned by Michael Jackson, then Controller of BBC2, with the intention of capturing a younger audience for the channel. (Lister: 3) Jackson, having moved to Channel 4 by 1999, wanted boundary pushing signature dramas of which *Queer as Folk* was a notable example (Miller and Jackson: 3).
10. The critiques of naturalism were most cogently developed by Georg Lukacs (Lukacs 1970). For a discussion of the problems and strengths of television naturalism, see Williams (1977).

References

Ang, I., 1985: *Watching Dallas, Soap Opera and the Melodramatic Imagination*, London, Methuen.

Baguley, D., 1990: *Naturalist Fiction – The Entropic Vision*, Cambridge: Cambridge University Press.

Brooks, P., 1995: *The Melodramatic Imagination – Balzac, Henry James and the Mode of Excess*, New Haven, Yale University Press.

Buckingham, D., 1987: *Public Secrets – EastEnders and its Audience*, London, BFI.

Caughie, J., 2000: *Television Drama – Realism, Modernism and British Culture*, Oxford, OUP.

Corner, J., 2000: 'Afterword: Framing the New' in Holmes, S. and Jermyn, D. (ed.), *Understanding Reality Television*.

Corner, J., 2002: 'Performing the Real', *Television and New Media*, 3: 3.

Ellis, J., 2002: *Seeing Things: Television in the Age of Uncertainty*, I.B. Tauris, London.

Geraghty, C., 1990: *Women and Soap Opera*, Cambridge, Polity Press.

Gledhill, C., 1987: 'The Melodramatic Field: an Investigation' in Gledhill, C. (ed.), *Home is Where the Heart Is*, London, BFI.

Halsted, N., 1997: 'Talking About My Generation', *The Independent*, April 14.

Higson, A., 1986: '"Britain's Outstanding Contribution to the Film" The Documentary Realist Tradition' in Barr, Charles, (ed.), *All Our Yesterdays*, London, BFI.

Holmes, S. and Jermyn, D. (eds), 2004: *Understanding Reality Television*, London, Routledge.

Lister, D., 1997: 'That's Death for *This Life*', *The Independent*, 7th August.

Lukacs, G., 1970: 'Narrate or Describe?' in Lukacs, G. *Writer and Critic*, trans. A. Kahn, London, Merlin.

Millar, S. and Jackson, J., 1999: 'Channel 4 glad to pioneer the first gay drama on British TV'. *The Guardian*, 24th February.

Moseley, R., 2002: 'Makeover takeover on British television', *Screen*, 41: 3.

Petley, J., 1996: 'Fact plus fiction equals friction', *Media, Culture and Society*, 18.

Sutcliffe, T, 1997: Television Review, *The Independent*, 8 Aug.

Williams, R., 1997: 'A Lecture on Realism'.

'I'VE BEEN SEARCHING MY SOUL TONIGHT'[1]: THE *ALLY MCBEAL* EFFECT

Jill Barker

In the United States the series *Ally McBeal*[2] was an undisputed overnight success, winning awards[3] and a substantial following of viewers. In the UK, on the other hand, its reception was deeply ambivalent and its broadcast history correspondingly fraught with false starts and re-scheduling.[4] Casual conversation revealed that, while there are many fans in the UK, dislike of the show was also widespread. This was expressed in generally visceral, intense and non-analytic terms: utterances such as 'erk', 'yuk' and 'I can't stand her' displayed its indigestibility and indicated a non-rational level of response.[5] Indeed, the very passion with which it was (and is) rejected reveals the psychic importance of the rejected object. Those who are fans of *Ally McBeal* are often similarly reluctant to accept analyses, and the nature of their responses could be freely explored on ephemeral Internet chatlines and message boards at the time when the show was being aired. Here, too, a clear distinction could be found between the interests expressed by American and British fans; the American group showing a strong preference for discussing the lives of the actors involved. The assumption was that the role performed and the actor performing the role were so intricately related as to be inseparable, and one message board contributor, when provoked, argued articulately against any separation. In the UK, on the other hand, plot lines and character development had a share in viewers' interests, alongside their interest in the actors.

This investigation probes the complex reactions of repugnance and laughter from two directions. The first selects portions of a wide-ranging questionnaire to explore the intellectual expectations and artistic preferences of those who react strongly to the series. The second and larger argument uses a literary critical approach to consider the programme's content, in particular its obsessive concern with the body as grotesque.

Inextricably, it also looks at the artistic techniques of distortion and surrealism used by the programme to explore that concern. The perspectives of order/disorder and control/chaos supply literary/psychoanalytic explanations for the intensity of the McBeal effect. These perspectives stem from concepts of carnival put forward by Mikhael Bakhtin[6] and of subjectivity developed by Jacques Lacan.[7] For simplicity, most of the examples used here refer to scenes and events in the first series.

The questionnaire (see Appendix) was completed by 36 mixed-age and mixed-gender groups of students in Media Arts and in English Literature at the University of Luton, between 2001 and 2003. As part of the exercise, they also viewed episode five of series 1 ('The Promise').[8] The questionnaire sought to prompt an analytic rather than a visceral response, but only a few respondents perceived the presence of multi-layered narratives or valued them. It seems, then, that many people switch off their professional lives when watching soaps and series.

The relationships between several questions were especially useful. Question 5, 'What are your personal criteria for a successful series or soap?', prompted respondents to analyse their tastes in viewing. Question 6, 'Have you watched Ally McBeal before?', was necessary in order to distinguish experienced viewers from those whose opinions were formed during the questionnaire. Question 7, 'Why did you stop?', and question 8, 'Why do you watch it?', are alternatives. Each uses an open multiple-choice technique plus a write-in section to suggest a range of possible reasons to the respondent, and so to explore the match between Ally McBeal and the respondent's criteria for a successful soap. Questions 1–4 inclusive make it possible to explore the respondent's viewing patterns and from that to make comparisons between those and attitudes to Ally McBeal. These questions explore the artistic context within which the respondent placed Ally McBeal, as does question 9, 'What expectations did you have?', and question 1, 'Were your expectations fulfilled?'. Questions 12–14 sought to probe whether viewers had noticed the time sequence from morning to evening in many of the episodes, and whether they had noticed that the content of the court cases was thematic in relation to the daily lives of the characters. (Some did notice the resemblance, but none saw the double plot as a way of engaging in dialogue over a moral/ethical debate.) Indeed, it is precisely the hesitations – the postponed decisions inevitably involved in debate – that attract some of the most scathing criticisms of the Ally character. Question 16, 'What is your opinion of the animation sections?', attempted to focus attention on the surreal aspects of the series and elicit discussion of the contribution that these make to the debates under way. The survey shows little difference in response between male and female respondents. It should be noted that results over this relatively small sample are indicative, rather than definitive.

Firstly, the answers to question 5 by regular viewers of the series were compared with those of irregular and non-viewers. The largest differences occurred in the area of plot and in two of the areas to do with characters: regular viewers were more likely to favour unusual characters (48 per cent versus 14 per cent) and somewhat less likely to perceive a strong plot as necessary (52 per cent compared with 78.6 per cent). They were also much less likely to assert a wish to identify with characters in a series (33.3 per cent compared with 64.3 per cent). In other words, viewers who sought to empathize tended not to choose 'Ally McBeal'. (I take the term 'identify' when used in common speech, as here, to be equivalent with 'relate to', and both terms to indicate a kind of empathy for the character: a sense that the character embodies aspects of personality or emotion or, indeed, of situation in life, which feel familiar to the speaker and which the speaker either has experienced or can envisage themselves as experiencing.) The desire to 'identify' with a character, as expressed by non-specialists, indicates a sense that what takes place on screen could be real. This is rather different from the 'willing suspension of disbelief' with which we are familiar, since this kind of viewer requires that disbelief *be suspended for* him or her by the events on the screen. A failure in credibility is therefore seen as a fault *in* the programme, and also as the fault *of* the programme. Such an expectation clearly is likely to be antipathetic towards most postmodern effects such as the mixing of narrative genres; collages of animation and photography; self-reflexivity; and apparently 'mad' characters. It is unsurprising then, that such values would accompany rejection and even incomprehension of 'Ally McBeal'. More surprising is the desire by such viewers for strong plots, since the plotting in *Ally McBeal* is exceptionally complex and detailed. Indeed regular watchers tended not to require a 'strong plot'. It may be that the phrase 'strong plots' was taken by respondents generally to imply simple, clear or linear plots, while complex or multiple narratives, though requiring tighter organization on the part of the writer, may be perceived as wayward or 'weak' by these viewers. This becomes clearer when one looks at the results for questions 5, 7 and 9.

Question 7 identified those who had ceased to watch the series. Of that group, 22 per cent asserted that the plot was confusing, while a further 22 per cent found the main character difficult to like and to 'identify' with. Question 8 revealed that a majority of people expected it to be funny, but this group could be divided further into those whose expectations were realized (62 per cent of the watchers and 50 per cent of the non-watchers); and those whose expectations were wholly disappointed by the sample episode (none of the watchers and 50 per cent of the non-watchers). The remainder of watchers gave the equivocal answer 'partly realized'. It would appear from this that in order to find the show funny a viewer must first like it enough to watch a number of episodes, rather than vice versa. Question 16 asked non-watchers about their response to a single episode. Write-in negative answers included: 'dull', 'unimpressive' and 'not funny', while positive responses were 'comic' and 'better than expected'.

The questionnaire, though interesting in itself, does not take us far enough in understanding what is taking place within *Ally McBeal*. Modes of literary criticism including the psychoanalytic and the Bakhtinian offer ways of interpreting both the series (now completed) and individual episodes. In this second approach, I begin from the sense that a short circuit of analysis swings into play in some viewers, located sometimes in a sense of personal identity. The respondents, like those mentioned above who 'can't identify with' or 'can't relate to' the characters, express an intangible quality of outrage, as if they, the viewers, were somehow personally insulted by the very presence of the series. Lisa Jardine[9] (who likes the programme) posits an explanation in terms of mirroring effects. Insecure female viewers in particular see their own insecurities uncomfortably reflected in the Ally character, and in repudiating her they repudiate an aspect of themselves that they do not wish to recognize.[10] Their frequent complaint, 'I can't relate to her', and the quality of revulsion actually mask an all-too-effective projection-relationship. This construction locates 'Ally McBeal'/Ally McBeal as an abjected other: an object cast away by the self, in order to protect the self's sense of completeness. Such an object functions both to 'screen' identity by hiding it (as behind a Chinese screen which itself only draws attention to the concealment) and to 'screen' identity by displaying it (as on a cinema screen).[11] For Jardine, viewers with more secure identities are less threatened by the McBeal hesitations, and so are free to enjoy the show, presumably as a comedy of embarrassment. Such viewers can thus externalize the inadequacies of the characters, making them into objects of observation. This view is borne out by the results to question 8 which show that of the occasional and regular viewers, 67 per cent value it for the plot and 71 per cent value it for the comedy, while only 4.8 per cent seek identification with the main character. Thus, regular viewers indeed do not identify with the McBeal character. Of the occasional and non-viewers, however, question 9 shows that very few had expected either a strong plot line (8 per cent) or sympathetic characters (17 per cent). Neither group, therefore, accepts that these characters might bear any direct connection with their own identities, and the conscious attitude they express towards the series boils down to whether or not one finds comedy of the ridiculous entertaining. Both the viewers and the non-viewers, then, can be described as projecting inadequacies away from themselves: some perform that by mocking the display of folly, others by finding it 'boring'. Thus, it seems that, tentatively, we might extend Jardine's analysis to include a much wider group than she anticipated.

On the other hand, intuitively persuasive as Jardine's explanation is when it deals psychoanalytically with the indecision of the Ally character, it is necessarily brief and so cannot address the content of the fantasy scenes, the surreal visual effects or the series' obsessive interest in the body. The distinctive complexities of the narrative techniques also require attention, particularly since it would seem that very few viewers notice them. Cutting regularly between numerous short scenes is characteristic of soaps, as a method of tracing discrete plot lines simultaneously. It may be that familiarity with this technique generates a misreading of the thematic sub-plots in *Ally McBeal*.

It scarcely needs to be demonstrated that *Ally McBeal* is profoundly interested in the body as grotesque: the comedy of the lower parts is present from the opening quasi-scatological childhood reminiscence about smelling Billy's bottom, through the broad spectrum of clients and colleagues who pass through the series: large, small, sweating and twitching, human bodies variously collapse, leap, dance and sing. The narrative rationalizes their inclusion on ethical grounds – not only is the firm of Cage and Fish socially responsible, but the series, too, lays claim to social concern. As early as episode

2 of series 1, John Cage asserts a problematic negotiation between the concept of 'indecency' (here equivalent to soliciting) on one hand and 'decency' (marriage) on the other. These two are mediated by the law, perceived by Cage as an irritating obstacle to the desires of the body and articulated in a frank carnivalesque discourse. For a lawyer to perceive the law in these terms invokes the Lacanian conceptualization of the Law of the Father, as that which both prevents the satisfaction of desire, and enables the linguistic and other structures of civilized life.[12]

The deformation of bodies, however, aggregates inexorably as series follows series. Ally appears as a miniature version of herself when she feels diminished or embarrassed (pilot episode; series one episode 1; and others). Even without that exaggeration, Ally (or is it Calista Flockhart?) goes through worryingly thin phases, a detail detected when she is described as 'Skipper'[13] by a legal opponent. Over time Ally's flatmate, Renée, appears to possess steadily inflating bosoms: part of a 'breasts' theme that is initiated when Ally sees her mirror image as better endowed (pilot episode) and further articulated in Elaine's bizarre inventions – first, the 'face-bra' and then the mechanically jiggling bra. Further examples are too numerous to mention. We are compelled to look more closely at the phenomenon that this parade of non-standard bodies represents.

Ally McBeal treats bodies as tragi-comic objects. A kind of giggling horror is encouraged when, for example, the fat solicitor, Harry, collapses in slow motion (series 1, episode 5). He falls as if he was a gigantic tree, with rippling aftershocks, themselves intruding their comic effect into the serious world. To be precise, the collapse is not quite like that of a tree: rather, the representation of the fall quotes the techniques of children's natural history programmes, where a tree is felled in slow motion and bounces slightly as it settles to the ground. Harry's fall is thus invested both with an impressive magnitude and with a joking reference to a shared visual experience from all viewers' childhoods. Ally, horrified, acts out our awe, but immediately undercuts any sense of profundity by awkwardly facing the physical (and social) realities of mouth-to-mouth resuscitation. Her pale legs gangle childishly – inadequate angular shapes against the mass of Harry's upholstered dark suiting. As so often, however, Ally's risible attempts at correct behaviour are surprisingly successful. Once the resuscitation is completed, she re-incorporates her social and ethical act into physicality by remembering it in terms of a taste of onions. "The grotesque body is not separated from the rest of the world. It is not a closed, completed unit; it is unfinished, outgrows itself, transgresses its own limits. The stress is laid on those parts of the body that are open to the outside world...".[14] This scene offers in miniature a theme that persists in the programme, that of performing a balancing act between the structures of propriety, a sophisticated capacity to see the ridiculous, and a subversive urge to deny structures by reverting to chaotic physicality. That three-way negotiation can be located again and again, achieved by collapsing together authority and subversion and naughtily forcing them to co-exist in a warm glow of carnival laughter.

The fictional courtroom offers a world where these three are brought together. Of the rituals inverted in the programme, the judicial process is most prominent, where a preposterous courtroom parodies the expected precision of the law. Judges are incapable of keeping order and even actively contribute to disorder, as when one elderly judge ('Happy' Boyle) insists on examining the state of counsels' teeth, as if they were horses (series 1, episode 1). In this world Ally McBeal can avoid being disciplined by the Board of Bar Overseers because that would involve them in listening to a discourse they see as nonsensical: 'You'd no doubt appeal, and we'd be faced with seeing you and hearing you and all these people again. As deterrents go I can think of none more effective.' (series 1, episode 4) Thus, even at this early stage in the life of the programme, rationality supports an irrational conclusion by the forces of authority. When the Board is swayed by its own self-interest, or when a genre-bending jury sings along with John Cage's tricks, carnival as chaos has invested these solemn processes. Nevertheless, it is through these carnivalesque procedures that manifestly just (if unlikely) decisions are generated. In this chiasmic relationship, therefore, legal formality is demonstrated to be inherently embodied and so laughable, while chaos contains the structures of a natural justice. This is very different from carnival as the inversion of ritual, which is also frequent in *Ally McBeal*. In the latter, the preposterous courtroom parodies the normal processes of the law, and judges substitute their own arbitrary versions of order.

Indeed, the regularly repeated image of Ally McBeal walking to and from the office displays the three-way opposition of structure, subversion and the chaotic body. In series one we see her in a fashionable version of a severely tailored business suit, which images structure but at the same time denies itself by means of the microscopically short skirt. A short skirt normally indicates physical attractiveness, but in this case implications of sexuality are again denied by the body it makes visible: stick-like straight legs and heavy shoes look ready to stumble. The office world is invaded, not by sexuality, but by childhood, and this confusion of the childish and the sexual is furthered by a theme of perversity so recurrent and pervasive as to suggest the polymorphous perversity of childhood sexuality. Indeed, many of the storylines evolve around McBeal's idealistic – even immature – sexual values. Those fragile 'lower parts' (literally) of the legs and shoes could pitch their wearer out of the social world at any instant. She does indeed stumble several times. It is that instability of the illusion of control that makes Ally McBeal into an *Alice through the Looking Glass*[15] figure.

Others are displayed as bodies by the way in which the plot lines focus on people not just as selves, but as embodied selves. It thus exposes, and brings to consciousness, the ontological clash between that silent hegemony of perfect bodies over imperfect that is implicit in much of the visual media and the idealistic belief that bodies are irrelevant to who a person 'really' is. The key activity for many of these bodies is to regard themselves in the mirror, in the unisex toilet. To gaze into the mirror at Cage and Fish is to move between the Imaginary and Symbolic orders of Lacanian theory. For example, the shy, stammering John Cage can use the mirror to view himself as having the confidence of a Barry White. But where the Lacanian mirror phase offers the viewer a falsely organized image of him/herself, in *Ally McBeal* the mirror may support, but it may equally readily destroy one's self-image.[16] Ally uses it to compare herself with the apparently organized beauty of the other women and perceives a chaos of inferior hair, teeth and body parts generally. One may go so far as to see the unisex washroom as the central image of the series. Here conventional, gendered bodily privacy is (by definition) intruded on and so represented as fragile. The unisex functions in relation to the verbal in the same way as it does with the physical: confidences are overheard, often inadvertently and always embarrassingly. Here, then, both the body and the mind are in danger of exposure to the view of others. Because the unisex is both a narrative pivot and also a device that pares away psychic defences, the emotional is cross-cut with the rational in one of the programme's most subtle effects.

Such intersections are fundamental to Mikhael Bakhtin's theories when he writes of the body in its social context and of the functions of the carnivalesque. The carnivalesque is characterized by three prominent effects, onto which the obsessions of *Ally McBeal* can be mapped. These are inverted ritual; parodic or comic speech; and a focus on the lower parts.[17] Bakhtin's view of ritual, and of ritual overturned, chimes readily with Lacan's concept of the Symbolic (instituted by the 'Law of the Father') and its dynamic relationship with the activity of the Imaginary.[18] It is more than appropriate, then, that Ally learned about the law as a profession by watching her father at work in courtrooms when she was a child (pilot), that she challenges the structures of legal authority, and that these challenges are worked through in the context of noticeably absent parents. Structurally, they are unnecessary, as there are already ample 'parental' structures in the narrative of Ally's self-creation.

The rituals of the psychoanalyst's session and their inversion become thematic from series 2, episode 15 when Tracey Ullman plays Dr Tracy Clark, a self-obsessed, singing psychoanalyst. This eccentricity would be remarkable if the show had any pretensions to realism, but by the time of the second series, it is clearly parodic. While most inversions are parodies, not all parodies are based on inversion: frequently distortion is involved, but that can still be seen as a kind of 'uncrowning' of the object of the parody. When, for example, the myth of the beautiful young woman is juxtaposed against the programme's characteristic technique of realizing metaphor in such physical distortions as Elaine's 'swelled head' (pilot; episode 1) and the 'panting tongues' of sexual arousal (series 1: episode 7 and others), not only is the concept of beauty deposed, but the conventions of the TV series centred around a lovely female protagonist's relationships are upended. Some viewers have expressed themselves baffled by the show's refusal of that model. Flockhart is not conventionally 'beautiful', and I argue above that she can represent a childish energy and a childish moral weight, through which 'fairness' is appealed to with vigorously persuasive naiveté. Her thin form and disproportionately large eyes support that construction, allowing her to be a bearer to our culture of unwelcome truths about itself.

Parodic and comic speech abound, especially in John Cage's blurting stammer and uncontrolled spurts of speech; and in Richard Fish's tactless remarks. This is developed further in the plot line about a woman with Tourette's syndrome.[19] One should include the habitual use of music in this category of revelatory uncontrolled sounds, especially popular song, which appears unbidden (and sometimes unwanted) to underscore emotional events, and even to make callously satirical comments on them.[20]

I began by seeking to understand why this programme generates a particular kind of antipathy in some viewers. It now seems that psychoanalysis offers one possible answer, but does not address the difficulty that many viewers like the programme without quite seeing much of its complexity. If they do enjoy the carnivalesque qualities, it is without much sense of their implications, and insofar as the complexities feed enjoyment subliminally, then so far are they doing that from within the repressed. Neither the 'watchers' nor the 'non-watchers' detect the profundity of the moral debates, nor the war between structure and subversion that I have identified above. There was a special (and surprising) quality about the laughter I heard when screening an episode of *Ally McBeal* to the questionnaire respondents. It felt collective and slightly excessive, as if the laughter was at least partly generated by expectations about the piece, in turn obliging a reading of narrative events as broad comedy. Expectations were conditioning reactions and laughter was turning a collection of individuals into a group. Mocking laughter like this is not a solitary behaviour: it works best in crowds and involves a particular kind of group concept of what is funny. Here we have a hint that reactions to this programme may not be solely about the individual psyche. That mocking laughter is characteristically the sound of a group sharing its values. For the less confident individuals the psychoanalytic explanation is feasible, but those others who richly enjoy the show, reject McBeal's hesitations by mocking them and, hence, by objectifying them: rendering them external and other. This group, like the non-viewers, may be claiming a false integrity of subjectivity but using a different process.

By reading social structures as metaphoric of the Lacanian Symbolic, and conversely, seeing moments of Bakhtinian subversion as capable of representing the return of the repressed, I have consciously conflated two potentially diverse discourses. Bakhtin and Lacan seem to address similar issues, but this is true only at a rather general level. In fact Lacan's chaos/order are at the level of the individual psyche and are expressed as the Imaginary versus the Symbolic. For Bakhtin, subversion is a social activity, and directed through and at the socio-political structures within which we live. To find an explanation of the blindnesses of both those who mock and those who reject, the theories I have used so far need to be refracted differently. Gramsci's concept of social hegemony and consensus as interconnected yields a way of doing that.[21] Hegemony

> involves subduing and co-opting dissenting voices through the subtle dissemination of the dominant group's perspective as universal and natural, to the point where the dominant beliefs and practices become an intractable component of common sense.[22]

Consider for a moment the consequences of fully comprehending the critical relationship with authority that *Ally McBeal*'s carnival of manners debates so frankly.

Participating in that debate would involve a loss of consensus: that willing ignorance of moral problems that enables society to continue to subscribe to the values of hegemonic standards. Such ignorance includes a willingness to debate those values, but only in accustomed terms and with safe conclusions. Crucially, consensus may not examine belief structures too deeply, even though one of our founding beliefs is in the value of openness, frankness, free examination. The process of the law, in fact, as we believe it to be. *Ally McBeal*, try though it may, cannot force its viewers to move beyond that safe radicalism from which they may enjoy the conventionally outrageous discourses, and so feel daring and modern, while closing down to more profoundly disruptive aspects.

The negotiation in *Ally McBeal* is, thus, at several levels – between conflicted individual and unified identity; between conservative social structures and liberal permissiveness; and thirdly, perhaps, glimpsed as it flickers through the interstices of our own interpretative presuppositions, between the hegemonic rule/consensus system and genuine subversion.

Notes

1. Lyrics to the series' theme song, written and sung by Vonda Shepherd.
2. First screened 8th of September 1997; final episode screened 20th May 2002.
3. In 1997 it won Golden Globe Awards both for 'Outstanding Production' and for 'Leading Actress' in a musical or comedy series. Over the entire run, the programme achieved five Emmys and four Golden Globes, in addition to numerous nominations.
4. Not only was the timing of broadcasts changed at short notice, but the day of the week also varied. Channel 4 does not divulge its reasons for programming decisions, but the same effect can be seen in its treatment of other American series.
5. A 'spineless, confused, whinny twig' is how the 'Ally McSwill' website refers to the main character. On another site devoted to attacking various popular series, more than 92,000 correspondents have voted, displaying a range of envy, viciousness and resentment (www.whowouldyoukill.com/ally.html).
6. Mikhael Bakhtin, *Rabelais and His World*, tr. Helene Iswolsky (Indiana University Press, 1984), first published in Russian, 1965; the *Dialogic Imagination* (University of Texas Press, 1981).
7. Jacques Lacan, *Ecrits: a Selection*, tr. Alan Sheridan (Tavistock 1971), first published in French, 1966; *The Four Fundamental Concepts of Psychoanalysis* ed. Jacques-Alain Miller, tr. Alan Sheridan (London: Hogarth Press, 1977), first published in French, 1973.
8. Excellent synopsis of individual episodes can be found at http: //allymcbeal.tktv.net/.
9. Professor Lisa Jardine, Queen Mary University of London, verbal communication, April 2000.
10. Freud called this process 'projection'. The term has been widely adopted into ordinary parlance from psychoanalysis. 'Operations whereby qualities, feelings, wishes or even 'objects', which the subject refuses to recognise or rejects in himself, are expelled from the self and located in another person or thing' (J. Laplanche and J. B. Pontalis, tr. D. Nicholson-Smith, *The Language of Psychoanalysis* (London: Karnac Books and the Institute of Psychoanalysis, 1988), p. 349.

11. See Jill Barker, 'Screening the Other' in Literary Theories: A Reader and Guide ed. J. Wolfreys (Edinburgh: University of Edinburgh Press, 2000) pp. 201–210.

12. The Law of the Father can be explained as follows: 'Unless we accept some restrictions we cannot differentiate ourselves from our surroundings and so become fully human and aware. Such a distinction can only be made for us by an external force, since while the infant (or for that matter any person) is in the solipsistic state it cannot initiate a sense of self as distinct from a surrounding not-self. Acquiring a sense of self therefore involves the loss of that blissful oneness of early infancy, but in exchange of this burden of separation – of human being – comes a huge compensation in the form if a capacity to make patterns. Patterns conform to rules, and rules, once again, can only exist by virtue of saying 'no' to some possibilities...For both Freud and Lacan the first 'no-sayer' in a child's life is the father...who denies the child his previously absolute access to gratification...in doing so, he forces the child to leave behind its sense that it and the world together form a complete and undifferentiated whole, and to accept that a third term exists', p. 98 in Jill Barker, 'Does Edie Count?: a Psychoanalytic Perspective on "Snowed Up"' in Literary Theories: A Case Study in Critical Performance eds. J. Wolfrey and W. Baker (London: MacMillan, 1996, pp. 75–99).

13. Skipper is the name of a well-known Mattel doll: the pre-pubescent sister of the Barbie doll.

14. Mikhael Bakhtin, Rabelais and His World (first published in Russian, 1965) tr. Hélène Iswolsky (Indiana University Press, 1984), p. 26.

15. Carroll Lewis, Alice Through the Looking Glass (Puffin, 1972), first published 1872.

16. 'The Mirror stage as formative of the function of the I' in Jacques Lacan, Ecrits: A Selection, tr. A. Sheridan, first published in French in 1966.

17. Mikhael Bakhtin (1984), pp. 4–5.

18. Jacques Lacan, Ecrits: A Selection, tr. A. Sheridan, first published in French in 1966.

19. Series 4, episodes 9–15.

20. For example, in series 1, episode 7, Fish explains that he had wanted work at his firm to be fun. Ally reassures him that it is a 'party', and the scene cuts to Vonda Shepherd singing 'It's my party and I'll cry if I want'.

21. Antonio Gramsci, eds Quintin Hoare and Geoffrey Nowell-Smith Selections from the Prison Notebooks of Antonio Gramsci (1971).

22. Douglas Litowitz, 'Gramsci, Hegemony, and the Law' Brigham Young University Law Review (2000) p. 519.

Index